AF522122

EDUCATION AND DEVELOPMENT

A STUDY OF HUMAN CAPITAL FORMATION

EDUCATION AND DEVELOPMENT

A STUDY OF HUMAN CAPITAL FORMATION

By

Dr. K. Suman Chandra
Faculty Member
Centre for Social Development
National Institute of Rural Development
Hyderabad (Andhra Pradesh)
(India)

DISCOVERY PUBLISHING HOUSE PVT. LTD.
NEW DELHI-110 002

First Published - 1997
Reprinted - 2018

ISBN: 978-81-7141-379-9

© Author

Education and Development

Published by:
DISCOVERY PUBLISHING HOUSE PVT. LTD.
4383/4B, Ansari Road, Darya Ganj
New Delhi-110 002 (India)
Phone: +91-11-23279245, 43596064-65
Fax: +91-11-23253475
E-mail: discoverybooksindia@gmail.com
discoverypublishinghouse@gmail.com
namitwasan9@gmail.com
web: www.discoverypublishinggroup.com

Printed at:
Infinity Imaging Systems
Delhi

CONTENTS

Preface

The acquired capabilities of farm people play an important role in modernizing agriculture and also serve as means of production. But the acquired capabilities are not given at any particular time frame. Although skills and related knowledge can be improved and enhanced throughout life, there are strong cultural and economic reasons for acquiring most of them while young age. There is also the basic economic fact that acquired capabilities are nor free; they entile real, identifiable costs. They are, in essence, an investment in *human capital*. Investment in education and training to increase the efficiency of people, is most important.

The book emphasises the importance of education in improving the productive capacity of societies and their political, economic and scientific institutions. The central thesis for the study is that the investment in human capital in the major source of economic and social development. Rapid and sustained growth rests heavily on particular investments in farm people related to the new skills and new knowledge that farm people must acquire to succeed, for the high growth rate. Considerable level of skill is required in mulberry cultivation and cocoon rearing in using new knowledge and modern input materials. Therefore, it increases the quality of produce and at the same time, increases yields of crop and produces more per farm worker.

Many have contributed to this study report. I thank all the respondents who have given me their time, information and insights. They are many, and here nameless, but their contributions have been generous and fundamental. While it is difficult to acknowledg all of them individually, I would like to place on record my deep and sincere gratefulness for the following persons.

At the outset, I express my deep gratitude to Prof. Y.B. Abbasayulu, for his valuable advise and encouragement in carrying out this study. I wish to place on record my sincere thanks and gratitude to our former Director General Shri T.L.Sankar, IAS, and Present Dy.Director General Shri P.Vanamali, IAS (NIRD) without whose initiative and encouragement this study would not have seen the light of the day. I equally indebeted to Dr. R.R. Prasad and Dr. Rajgopal who have been in touch with this work since its inception. I was fortunate enough to have discussions with persons like Prof. G. Partha Sarathy, Shri R. Krishna Murthy, and Dr.R. Siva Prasad for the conceptual clarity of this work. I am very much thankful to all of them.

I am highly grateful to all my colleagues in the Centre for Social Development of National Institute of Rural Development. I extend my sincere thanks to my colleague Shri. P. Satish Chandra who helped me in data analysis. My thanks are also to many of my colleagues in other Departments of the Institute.

My Special Thanks to all my faculty friends who helped in one way or the other and extended their support viz., Dr. Y. Gangi Reddy, Dr. V. Annamalai, Shri G. Rajanikanth, Dr. Ommen John and Dr.E.V. Prakash Rao for their timely advise and sincere comments.

I will be failing in my duty if I do not record my deep sense of gratitude to various Officials in the villages who have cooperated with me in collecting data for this study.

I am also thankful to Miss Anitha Rani and Miss M.Bhagya Lakshmi who have taken keen interest in typing the report.

K. Suman Chandra

1
INTRODUCTION

"If you plan for a year, plant a seed. If for ten years, plant a tree. If for hundred years, teach the people. When you sow a seed once, you will reap a single harvest, when you teach the people, you will reap hundred harvests".

— K' UAN-TZU, 551-479 BC.

Education in Pre-Colonial India

In pre-colonial India, people of upper castes had the privilege of better education although in some regions like Kerala, people belonging to middle and low castes also had access to education to some extent. For the common people, there were in every village and town, vernacular schools which taught mainly reading, writing and rudiments of arithematic. These schools also imparted religious instruction to the pupil. These schools were generally taken advantage of by the some sections of the society and agriculturists hardly received any education. Thus, education among the commons, in Pre-British India, was extremely restricted and for all, except the elite, very poor in content and coverage.

Further, education as a part of the entire culture of the society, controlled and administered by the specific section, has been a mode of training. It taught the pupil the virtue of unconditional allegiance to elders, to parents, to teachers, to the king. In fact, education was a means of making the individual accept and conform to hierarchical structure of the society and completely subordinate his individuality to it.

Education During British Rule

The introduction of modern education was an event of great historical significance for India. It was definitely a progressive act of the British rule. Three main agencies were responsible for the spread of modern education in India. They were (*i*) Foreign Christian Missionaries; (*ii*) British Government and (*iii*) Progressive Indians.

The Christian Missionaries, who did extensive work in the sphere of the spread of modern education in India were inspired mainly by the proselytizing spirit to spread Christianity among the people. These missionaries started educational institutions which along with imparting modern secular education and also gave religious instruction in Christianity.

The British Government was however, the principal agent in disseminating modern education in India. It established a network of schools and colleges in India which turned out educated Indians versed in modern knowledge. The introduction of modern education in India was primarily motivated by the political, administrative and economic needs of Britain in India. However, there were other motives also. There were enlightened Britishers who were convinced that the spread of British culture would bring about a social and political unification of the world.

The third powerful effort in spreading modern education in India was endorsed by Indians themselves. Veteran leaders like Raja Ram Mohan Roy, Vivekananda, Gokhale, Malviya and others worked towards the establishment of modern education.

Modern education has fundamentally different orientation and organization as compared to traditional education. Its content is liberal and exotic and it is steeped in modern world view. Freedom, equality, humanism, spread of science and technology and denial of faith in dogmas are the themes which a modern education should contain. It has a professional structure which is not ascribed to any specific group of class but can be achieved by merit by any one in society. Some branches of modern education such as science directly focus on a world - view which embodies the core values of modernization and imparts skills to realize the goal of a modern society.

Thus, with the introduction of the modern system of education both meaning and content of education underwent significant changes. It became less religious and many new branches of learning were introduced. The printing press revolutionised the educational system in that the emphasis shifted from personal, oral communication to impersonal communication of ideas through books, Journals and other media. Modern education was also the medium for the spread of modern science and ideas of equality and liberty. Education became the prominent tool for exploiting new economic opportunities which were to a large extent caste-free. Further, educational opportunities helped in acquiring the necessary skills.

Education in Independent India

Education was regarded in the Constitution of Independent India as the democratic right of every citizen. Article 45 contained the following Directive of State Policy: "*The State shall endeavor to provide, within a period of ten years from the commencement of this Constitution, for free and compulsory education for all children until they complete the age of fourteen*".[1] The importance of education also expressed by the Indian National Commission, that education should be used as a powerful instrument of social, economic and political change[2]. It is widely believed that the rapid quantitative expansion of educational opportunities was the keystone to accelerate socio-economic development; it would contribute towards skill formation, increase in productivity, and learning of new ideas and techniques. Moreover, universal primary education would enhance the opportunities for social mobility of the poor and the underprivileged.

In recent years, the concept of education is beginning to be equated with learning, irrespective of where, when and how often it occurs. To get a clear picture of this learning - centred view, education can be grouped into three identifiable categories: formal, informal and non-formal education. Schooling and formal education refers to what is taught in school and other related institutions; informal education includes all forms of non-school experiences which socialize an individual into the customary mores of society and non-formal education refers to organised educational activity which occurs outside the school[3].

Review of Literature

Education and Development

Education in India has been recongised as the key input to development, yet the growth of education has been inadequate and largely centered in and around urban areas. The earlier attempts to study the economic aspects of education have also been confined to urban areas with scanty reference to rural areas and to issues like Crude Assessment of the Stock of Human Capital and Returns to Education. In the rural context pioneering work was done by Chaudhri[4]. His study covered workers and limited aspects of the economics of education, i.e., returns to education and impact of education on agricultural productivity and related attitudinal behaviour.

The role of education in the development sphere has been examined by different authors like Theodore Schultz, Frederick Harbison, Charles Myers, Bowman and Anderson, Denison, Chaudhri and others with (KAP) Knowledge, Attitude and Practice which are essential for accelerating the pace of development.

In modern economic thought, the concept of education as investment in human capital and as a critical factor in economic development is of recent origin. One may trace a clear trend of the indicative and causative factors for national development slowly shifiting from land as expressed by the physiocrates, to trade as propogated by the classical and neo-classical economists to innovations and entrepreneurship qualities as propounded by Schumpeter[5].

By the early 1970's, the prevailing view of development had widened, to the concern for greater production was added a concern for human welfare and the alleviation of poverty. Education came to be seen as a basic human need, as a means of meeting other basic needs, and as an activity that sustains and accelerates overall development. It is now generally recognised that development of a country's human resources is essential to its prosperity and growth and to the effective use of its physical capital. Education - investment in human capital - is an integral component of all development effort. It follows that education must cover a wide spectrum in content and in form, and that general education is as essential for the achievement of development objectives as training in specific skills[6].

Hence, education has been recognised as the key input to development. Education sector policy paper brought out by World Bank vividly described education as (*i*) a basic human need to acquire a broad base of knowledge, attitudes, values and skills provides to learn to respond to new opportunities, to adjust in political, cultural,economic and social activities;

(*ii*) means of meeting other basic needs, ultimately improving productivity and income; (*iii*) an activity that sustains and accelerates overall development as it prepares and trains skilled workers at all levels to manage capital, technology, services and administration in every sector of the economy and facilitates the advancement of knowledge in pure and applied fields[7].

Education improves the productive capacity of societies and their political, economic and scientific institutions. It also helps reduce poverty by mitigating its effects on population, health and nutrition and by increasing the value and efficiency of the labour offered by the poor. As economies world wide are transferred by technological advances and new methods of production that depend on a well-trained and intellectually flexible labour force, education becomes even more significant[8]. The future development of the world and of individual nations hinges more than ever on the capacity of individuals and countries to acquire, adapt, and advance knowledge. This capacity depends, in turn on the extent to which the population has attained literacy, education and problem-solving skills. To move forward, especially developing countries must improve the education and training of the labour force.

The concept of education is generally misconceived as equivalent to literacy. Literacy is to be perceived only as a tool to promote education. Throughout the developing world there prevailed conventional belief that there is a causal connection between the literacy rate and the pace of development.

Education helps to alleviate poverty and advance economic and social development. A plethora of research studies and literature demonstrates that the adults who have higher levels of educational attainment have more paid employment, higher individual earnings, greater agricultural productivity, lower fertility, better health and nutritional status, and more modern attitudes than adults who have lower educational attainment. They are also more likely to send their children to school. These characteristics are dimensions of development. It also forges national unity and social cohesion by teaching common mores, enhances the status of women, and promotes adaptability to technological change[9].

These ideas precipitated an increase in realization on the part of the policy makers that the modern agricultural development is dependent on the levels of education of the farmers. There is an overwhelming evidence supporting the fact that the development of agriculture is more dependent upon the ability, cognitive competence, management, adoptability to changing circusmstances, scientific and technological outlook of the farmer than of the so called traditional factors of production.

The nobel laureate Theodore Schultz[10] while studying the process of modern agricultural development focussed that *the main difference between a traditional agriculture and a modern one lies in the use of different factors of production: the former uses traditional factors of production which have been in existence for a long time while the latter use modern ones which keep changing in form as time goes by. Therefore, the problem of modern agricultural development is how to increase the supply of modern factors of production and how best farmers adopt and implement in their farms. This is possible through effective system of extension methods and level of schooling among the farmers.*

Schultz[11] also emphasised the importance of education and training which he considered to be forms of capital accumulation in socio-economic development. The productive capacity of human beings was vastly larger than other forms of capital and therefore, investment in human beings in the form of education, training in skills etc., was the most useful form of capital accumulation. He also emphasised that human resource was the ultimate basis of the wealth of nations, as it was people who accumulated capital, exploited natural resources, built social, political and economic organizations creating economic development.

In another pioneering study by Schultz[12] showed that investment in education creates human capital and in the United States of America, a substantial part of the unexplained increase in income between 1929 and 1956 represented a return to education in the labour force. Further, he argued against underrating human capital and overrating land and physical capital in the process of economic development. In his Nobel Lecture[13], the Economics of Being Poor, he observed, "*The decisive factors of production in improving the welfare of poor people are not space, energy and crop land; the decisive factors are the improvement in population quality, advances in knowledge*".

Professor Mellor[14] (1966) holds the similar point of view. He stressed the need to develop agriculture in such a way as to exploit the large quantity of underutilized resources already existing in agriculture like the unskilled labour, the land, the capital, and the capital formation potential of the economy by increasing profitable and efficient use of new and improved factors of production.

Rostow[15] emphasised that "the rate of growth of any economy is a function of the rate of change in the stock of capital including the stock of knowledge". Marshal[16] not missing the importance of this key factors, long back, observed: capital consists a great part of knowledge and organization. "Knowledge is the most powerful engine of production". Dobb[17] finds no other but "education, knowledge and skills" as the limiting factors in the process of development.

Development economist Arthur Lewis[18] described that knowledge was the most proximate cause of development. Alex Inkeles[19] who studied the process of "Becoming Modern" found that development required a transformation in the every nature of man. He attributed education as one of the charactristics of modern man. Of two people, both economically deprived, one will make sure that his child goes to school, the other will take the child out and put him in the work. From the point of view of the author, the one who keeps his child in school is taking a more modern course of action.

Denison[20] attributed to education 23 per cent of the growth in total national income and 42 per cent of the growth in per capita income over the period 1929-1957. Bowman and Anderson[21] arrived at some stage interesting conclusions on the role of education in development. Firstly, a 40% adult literacy is necessary though not a sufficient condition for economic development. Secondly, primary schooling is much more important for creating a base for development. Thirdly, public policy relating to education is critical. Japan's economic development and its spectacular recovery after World War II, is rightly attributed to the human factor as represented by her educated and trained manpower.

A study by the Japanese Ministry of Education[22] that was based on the analytical technique devised by Theodore Schultz indicated that though in 1960, the value of the stock of educational capital was 18 per cent of the value of the stock of physical capital, it yielded proportionately greater return. From 1930 to 1955, investment in education contributed a significatnt part of total increase in national income in Japan. The diffusion of elementary education improved the quality of the Japanese people's skills, modernised their thought and enabled them to participate successfully in modern economic activities. By 1915 Japan accomplished universal enrolment in elementary education and stress was laid on expansion of secondary education.

The rapid recovery of Japan from socio-economic collapse after World War II and its subsequent prosperity were made possible through the accumulated efforts of pre-war education. The successful role played by education in economic development in Japan should be attributed to the efforts of the people who had restricted even consumption and invested money on education.

Alva Myrdal[23] in a perspective article described the power of education in contributing to the early development of Sweeden and Denmark. Sweeden was fortunate enough to get universal literacy through compulsory schooling covering the total population half a century before the country was seriously drawn into the orbit of industrial civilization. The remarkable revolution in Denmark, particularly by the development of co-operative methods, starting with the second half of 19th century was rendered possible only because the Denmark popualtion was already rather thoroughly prepared by education. No other country had so early and so comprehensively instituted compulsory schooling.

Nalla Goundan[24] attributed slow rate of development of India to low rate of growth of human capital. He estimated that during 1950 - 61 the human capital in India increased by 48 per cent as against 71 per cent increase in the physical capital. This is in contrast with advanced countries where human capital has been growing at a much faster rate than the physical capital. For instance, in Japan the human capital increased three-times faster than the physical capital, and in the U.S.A. the increase has been 1.7 times more than the physical capital. The percentage share of the human capital in physical capital in Japan increased from 5.3 per cent in 1905 to 24 per cent in 1955; in the U.S.A. from 22 per cent in 1900 to 42 per cent in 1957; and in India it decreased from 26.1 per cent in 1951 to 14.6 per cent in 1961. The price of this neglect and ill planning is subjugation of masses to untold humiliation and sufferings.

Thus human capital formed by education has proved to be an active agent of economic growth. In the United States, in the U.S.S.R, in Japan and in Europe the Productive value of educational investment was found to be higher than that of physical capital for the periods under study.

It is with this perspective of development process that the importance of education and training for modern agricultural development especially in sericulture is recognised and emphasised. In order to absorb new and scientific agricultural inputs and management skills in sericulture, well educated manpower is necessary. World Development Report[25] emphasised investment in education and its direct effect on individual productivity and earnings.

It is interesting that most of the evidence comes from agriculture. Studies comparing the productivity and innovativeness of schooled and unschooled farmers in low income countries showed that, when inputs such as fertilizers and high-yielding seed varieties were available for improved farming techniques, the annual output of a farmer who had four years of schooling averaged 13 per cent higher than that of a farmer with no schooling. Even when these inputs were lacking, the schooled farmer's output was 8 per cent higher than the unschooled farmers.

A poor system of education compromises the entire system of human capital development. Most important, it does not produce enough truly educated parents, workers and managers who can contribute to development. To counter the above situation, educational effectiveness should improve means increasing the number of schools whose people master the core knowledge and skills of the curriculum. Most education systems in developed and in upper-middle-income developing countries graduate between 80–100 per cent of the students who enter primary school.

Although poor quality of education exists at all levels, improvement must begin at the primary level, where children develop their basic attitudes and approaches to learning. Improving the quality of education is a prerequisite for developing the human resource base required to meet the changing technological demands of the twenty-first century. To initiate a deeply rooted and sustainable process of technological development, human capital formation must be broadly based and allow a progressively larger share of the general population to participate in the process of socio-economic transformation.

The First Five Year Plan document emphasised, "*the problem of development of an underdeveloped economy is one of utilizing more effectively the potential resources available to the community, and it is this which involves economic planning. But the economic condition of a country at any given time is a product of the broader social environment, and economic planning has to be viewed as an integral part of a wider process aiming not merely at the development of resources in a narrow technical framework adequate to the needs and aspiration of the people*".[26]

The Prime Minister of India in his foreword to Seventh Five Year Plan has emphasised in the following words. "*In the final analysis, development is not just about factories, dams and roads. Development is basically about people. The human factor, the human context, is of the supreme value. We must pay much greater attention to these questions in future. The seventh plan proposed bold initiatives in these areas. Outlays for human resource development have been substantialy increased, policies and programmes in education, health and welfare must also be reconstructured to provide a fuller life for our people*"[27].

This point of view has been stated very early in the Seventh Five Year Plan "*A narrow view of resource mobilisation limiting it to the financial sphers, fails to do justice to the complexity of the development process in which the human factor plays the most significant part. Without adequate development of human resources in its widest sense we cannot avoid setbacks to the process of development itself. The productive forces of the economy can be strengthened only by releasing the creative energies of all strata of society*"[28].

Therefore, the human factor is an important correlate of socio-economic development. Productivity is not a simple consequence of economic resources and inputs. Economic resources are manipulated by the human factor which serves as a critical variable between input - output analysis. It has been realised that economic development per se is not the goal of a society. It is only a means to obtain necessary conditions for the development of the potentialities of human beings.

Education—Agricultural Development

Several studies have shown the substantial contribution of education to agricultural development. Low level of schooling of farm people is shown to be a limiting factor in the rate of agricultural development as poor countries begin to modernise their agriculture. Education is a crucial factor in the development and application of new technology to agriculture. In agriculture, trained manpower breaks the bottleneck to efficient utilization of the labour and land resources.

Farmers earnings provide an indirect measure of productivity, but physical productivity is the best measure of education's economic impact. Farmers with more education are physically more producitive than those with less. The effect of education on agricultural production can be assessed by comparing the agricultural output of farmers with different levels of educational attainment. Lockheed, Jamison, and Lau[29] summarised the findingsof eighteen studies containing thirty one data sets from thirteen developing countries. *They concluded that four years of primary education increased the productivity of farmers by 8.7 per cent overall and 10 per cent in countries undergoing modernization (largely in Asia). Education increased the ability of farmers to allocate resources efficiently and enabled them to improve their choice of inputs and to estimate more accurately the effect of these inputs on their overall productivity.*

Schultz[30] viewed that primary schooling is the most profitable of all. It entails the lowest costs per year of schooling when children are still too young to do any appreciable amount of useful farm work. There are rarely any earnings foregone on the part of the children from ages six to ten. The benefits accrue in part to the student and his family and in part they are captured by others. Literacy has a pervasive value in reducing costs and in improving the productive of the economy. When farm people are effectively literate the costs of producing and distributing new technical and related economic information are reduced very substantially.

Wharton[31] pointed that "the fundamental problem of agricultural growth is an educational problem". Particularly before the take-off stage of the economy, education does play a significant role. A few studies on rate of return to education have also been made with respect to agricultural workers.

Welch[32] studied the problem with the United States data concluded that, education influencing allocative ability and this plays a key role in determining education's productivity in agriculture and is more relevant in a dynamic setting. He also found that there is a significant positive relation between the years of schooling and incomes of the farm labour force in United States both for whites and non-whites.

Bowman[33] had argued that education and information relevant to the small farmer might usefully be categorised along a continuem, the poles of which she lables "Formation of competences - literacy, numeracy and general cognitive skills" are best formed through schools or similar institutions. Information on prices, new seeds or techniques, irrigation methods and so forth can be transmitted through a variety of institutional or non-institutional frameworks, including extension services whereas the goals of information transfer services can be stated in narrowly economic terms. The development of competence can be expected to have not only economic benefits in agriculture but also in the improvement of other aspects of household life and in the encouragement of a critical self-reliance.

Recent works suggested that primary education can have positive effects on farmer productivity—a possibility previously neglected. The work of Lockheed[34] *et.al*, suggested that—

(a) in four-fifths of the cases examined (in 13 low income countries) the relationship between years spent in school and agricultural output was positive;

(b) the most important determinant of whether education positively affects output or whether the farmer has any access to modern inputs—eg: new equipment and crop varieties - that education only operates as part of package.

Chaudhari[35] found from production function analysis that education is having a significant impact on agricultural productivity. He also finds that the level of education influences the use of new inputs like chemical fertilizers and machines in agriculture. He classified the various economic effects of education on agricultural development into four groups viz., (1) innovative effect (2) allocative effect (3) worker effect and (4) externality effect.

1. Innovative Effect

a) ability to decode new information, know—what, why, where and how;

b) ability to evaluate costs and benefits of alternatives; and

c) ability to establish the quickest access to newly available and economically useful information.

2. Allocative Effect

The allocative effect relates to improvements in production activity and business activity. The farmer's ability to choose optimum combination of crops and agricultural practices is improved through education. His ability to choose optimum time for marketing, transportation etc., is also improved as a consequence of education.

3. Worker Effect

The worker effect relates to improvement in labour productivity and ability to produce more from a given level of inputs.

4. External Effect

Education creates external economies in so far as the educated help the neighbouring farmers with access to information to improved practices etc. Thus the role of education is clearly recognised and is accepted as an important variable in explaining agricultural productivity.

Education effects productivity in two distinct ways the *allocative effect* and the *worker effect*. The former distinction centres on better allocation decisions including adoption and diffusion of new technology, while the latter relates to a more efficient use of given inputs i.e. the technical efficiency aspect of production. The allocative effect is inherently predicated on disequilibrium (e.g. change in technology) while there is some evidence to suggest that even the worker effect of education is more likely to arise during disequilibrium caused by technical change renders the existing cultural practices obsolete or inadequate and calls for an adjustment. A more educated person is supposed to make the required adjustment more quickly, establishing the above hypothesis.

Precisely, primary postulate of the allocative hypothesis is that education enhances the productive capabilities of persons by helping them to choose more optimum set of factors, efficient output mix and an appropriate scale. Such combination will add to enhance productivity potential of farmers. The optimal factor referred as above, stress the role of information in allocative decision and mentions the possible usefulness of schooling in relation to receiving and decoding information. However, an explicate postulate relating education, information, allocative efficiency and productivity is to be worth examine in sericulture which needs acquired capabilities.

Education also affects production by developing analytic modes of problem solving. Cotlear[36] found that education increases the ability of farmers to think abstractly, which enabled them to recognise the causal relation between technology and output. An example of this comes from Eisemon's[37] survey of farmers in Kenya, which examined the effect of primary education on the cognitive skills of farmers. Data were obtained from heads of households who had not been to school and from those who had completed upto seven years of primary education; both men and women were surveyed. Farmers who had been to school were able to construct causal models of events in the natural world and to demonstrate how these events could be controlled by humans. They were able to observe, diagnose, and correct common agricultural problems better than farmers with few years of education. They actively sought to solve problems, while unschooled farmers did not.

Adamski[38] considered education as a means of dissimination of information and his study revealed that the adoption of improved methods is quicker among farmers who are subscribing to a paper or a journal or those who read books on agricultural production in comparision to those who do not do so.

Harker, Bruce Rogers,[39] testing an analytical model of the relationship between education, communication behaviour, agricultural innovations and agricultural production, examined inter household and inter community data. *The study revealed that the number of times a farmer consults an agricultural extension agent in a year is related positively to his educational attainments than that of his father.*

Rati Ram[40] reported in his study that there is an effort towards identifying and understanding the role of education in production. Since it is proposed that the major effect of schooling operates through increased information, the value of schooling would be related to the value of information. To the extent that information is more valuable in an economic setting, schooling is likely to have a larger pay-off. Thus, by identifying situations in which information may be expected to be more valuable, one can locate the circumstances that make education more worthwhile. For instances, information and thus schooling might have greater value in "*dynamic*" production situations than in "*static*" environments. Another aspect studied in this study is of the possible difference between the value of information to farm operators and to farm hands hired for performing specific routine tasks. It seems likely that production—related information is more valuable to farm operators who take the relevant input-output decisions than to hired hands, the former have allocative functions to perform, while the latter typically do not.

Another study by Pudasaini[41] established the education's contribution to agricultural production through both worker and allocative effects. According to him the allocative effect was more crucial than the worker effect. Education enhances agricultural production mainly by improving farmer's decision-making ability and only secondarily by alleviating their technical efficiency in both the environments. The implication that emerges from these findings was that agricultural efficiency and productivity can be accelerated by simultaneously investing in education and in moderrn innovations.

Rate of return studies are generally undertaken to establish the relationship between education and productivity. A number of studies have also been undertaken in India. Gisser[42] estimated the rate of returns to education in agriculture and it is more than 20 per cent in any region in the United States. He finds that schooling in rural farm areas have two effects.

(1) The "out-migration" reducing the supply of human agents, and

(2) The "capability effect' increasing the productivity of labour and the net effect of more schooling would be to increase income or rural farm areas in addition to encouraging more farm out-migration. An increase in the level of schooling in rural areas by 10 per cent induces 6 to 7 per cent additional migration out of agriculture, and the net effect is a rise in agricultural productivity, resulting in a rise in the farm wage rate by 5 per cent.

Venkatasubramanian[43] has estimated private and social rates of return to primary and middle levels of education in Tamil Nadu basing on the NSS data relating to 1970-71 on earnings. He estimated that primary education yields a private rate of return of 39.6 per cent over illiterates and a social rate of return of 22.4 per cent respectively. In case of middle levels of education private rate of return is 14.2 per cent and social rate of return is 11.1 per cent. (Thus primary education is found to have a much higher private rate of return). The study conducted in low income countries[44], including India shows that the "mean gain in production for 4 years of education was about 6.4 per cent and that a number of studies showed evidence of a threshold number of years (4–6) at which the impact of education became more pronounced.

Thus, education generally has the effect of lowering the costs of acquiring production related information. Such lowering of marginal costs may occur for a variety of reasons, including the improved communication skills of more educated, persons, and the possible superiority of their contacts. The raise of marginal benefits could similarly be rationalised through the consideration that higher schooling probably sharpens the Judgemental faculties of persons and increase their capacity to process and apply the received information. Thus, by lowering marginal costs and raising marginal benefits, schooling is likely to increase the rate of acquisition of useful information by procedures, and such an increase in information acquisition is likely to constitute a major source of higher allocative and productive efficiency among more educated producers.

Education and Social Change

Education as the most important correlate of development was acknowledged at home and outside by social scientists. Numerous studies have shown positive correlation between education and modernity, believed to be the pre-requisite for development.

The Indian Planning Commission, while preparing the Third Five Year Plan in 1961–62, believed that education to be the most important single factor for economic development as well as social emanicipation. The report of the Education Commission, headed by Prof. Kothari,[45] titled Education and National Development which displayed its belief that education is the key to development. This report has reiterated that for social change and development there is one instrument and one instrument only, that is "Education".

The studies of modernization in developing countries showed that education was the most powerful force in shaping a man's modernity score. Education was generally two or three times as powerful as any other single input. Occupational experience and mass-media exposure shared the second rank more or less equally.

Numerous studies have proclaimed positive association of education with social change (Majumdar[46], Bhatia and Gupta[47], Rudolph and Rudolph[48]). Inkeles and Smith[49] in their study on "The Role of Industrialization in Modernization" found that education as a more powerful correlate of modernity than industrialization-urbanization.

Analysing the Indian data of the Harvard Project, Singh[50] examined the relative influence of education, caste, ethnicity, occupation and place of residence on modernity and found that education was the most important correlate of modernity. Singh[51] in his study of comparision of farmers, rural and urban factory workers, also found education to be the most important correlate of modernity.

A study in Bihar[52] showed that each additional year spent in school contributed to individual modernity. Only 2 per cent of those with no schooling at all featured in terms of their overall modernity score. The corresponding figures were 21 per cent, 28 per cent and 77 per cent for those who had 5, 8, and 11 years of schooling respectively. The people who had been in school longer were not only better informed and verbally more fluent. They had a different sense of time and stronger sense of personal and social efficacy, participated more activily in social affairs, and they were open to new ideas, new experiences, and new people interacted differently with others, and showed more concern for sub-ordinates and minorities. They valued science more, accepted change more and prepared to limit the number of children they would have. In short, by virtue of having more formal schooling, their personal character was decidedly more modern.

UNICEF[53] literature stated that literacy remains a primary issue for the majority of the female population among many developing countries. Illiterate mother plays a part in linking the chain of illiteracy to the next generation. It is also recognised that illiteracy prolongs women's dependence and subordination by cutting them off from participation in change, and further as modernization spreads, illiteracy comes to be despised more than the past, thus eroding women's economic status and self-respect. Thus, education not only improves the status of women, but will have a marked impact on the welfare of their families and the nation.

A study in Brazil[54] showed that at any given income level, the feeding is positively related to mother's education. Similarly in Kerala at a given level of income, the ability to allocate food items in such a way as to meet minimal requirements improve with the level of education. This signifies the role that literacy can play in minimizing the magnitude of under nutrition.

A study in 29 developing countries[55] showed that infant and child mortality rates are lower when the mother's level of schooling is higher. It is evident that maternal education not only reduces child mortality but also improves the health of the survivors and hence children of more schooled mother tend to be better nourished.

A study of primary education, population growth and socio-economic change[56] indicated that the educational expansion in Kerala in the past several decades indicated contrary to the prevailing view among educational planners in many parts of the world, economic backwardness need not be necessary at as an insuperable barrier to the spread of mass primary education, provided the initiative and the enthusiasm necessary for such a process to take place emanate from the people themselves. Once this basic condition is satisfied, perhaps no country will find itself so poor as to deny primary education to its people.

Another study in Kerala by Panikar[57] showed that low crude death rates and infant mortality rates and higer life expectancy at birth rate in Kerala are attributed to diffused awareness and utilization of health facilities. The phenomenon in turn has been attributed to a fairly wide spread utilization of educational facilities and established tradition of ensuring around total enrolment and retention of both boys and girls in primary schools.

Therefore, Panikar in his study concluded that: the high level of literacy and education among females in Kerala is the one factor which has contributed most to the improvement of the health status of infants and children. The spread of education among women in the rural parts of Kerala was probably a crucial factor contributing to the high degree of awareness of health problems and fuller utilization of the available health care facilities.

Thus Kerala's achievement in social progress has been attributed to diffused primary educational facilities throughout the state (unlike the rest of India) and retention of girls in middle school stage and also for about four years of primary schooling on an average.

A study by Operational Research Group (ORG)[58] showed a linkage between female literacy and family planning. It indicated that a large proportion of the couples where wife had gone to primary school were more aware and less resistant to family planning measures, and expressed a desire for fewer children. Proportionately more of the couples where the wife was illitereate disapproved of adopting birth control methods to delay or prevent pregnancies. Increased practice of family planning was associated proportionately more with couples where either or both spouses had gone to primary school as compared to matched illitereates.

The sociological and psychological studies in India have concluded that there is a positive relationship between education and to the indices of social change, modernity and development. The indices includes aspirations, need for achievement, rationality, competence, openness to change, acceptance of family planning, social equality and political consciousness.

Education and Sericulture

Sericulture being an agro-based rural industry is highly suitable to the countries having an agricultural base and problems of providing employment to the rural landless labourers. In fact, the silk production has brought advantages to small and marginal farmers in developing countries. It is mainly rural and labour intensive industry, requires relatively low investment and offers high profit potential and foreign exchange earnings. Mulberry leaf which is a feed to silkworms could be raised using the land unsuitable for other crops while wastage by-products from sericulture can be of good value. The silkworm which has been domesticated and evolved over many thousands of generations, to produce substantial quantities of silk in a very short period is indeed very delicate and requires careful handling during the process of rearing. Therefore, the job of rearing highly productive silkworms in tropical areas as in South India is really tough.

Management concept is one of the crucial input required for optimum utilization of resources, namely men, money and mechines in different time frame, as there are always scarce and can easily be put to better alternative uses, Hence, their optimum utilization becomes more important in the larger interests of the society. One cannot even dream of utilizing resources in an optimum manner without proper management, as in the process wastage as well as misappropriate utilization are bound to occur,such irregularities at times are very large and surely become detrimental to the interests of the farmers. This precisely, the main reason for managerial inputs gaining importance in sericulture.

How can a farmer conceptualise an intelligent view of input and output management or their relation to productivity and profits without the knowledge or basic education that can give? How can without such education one can achieve higher productivity or income? How can an extension worker succeed in introducing innovative programmes if the people with whom he come into contact are of the category of illiterates? These are the some of the important questions that need to answered if countries productivity has to be raised in any field/sector. The people, whom we are expecting to increase production if they are not in a position to learn and discuss among themselves, no transformation is possible in the system. This can only be possible if primary education becomes compulsory and reorient to the pressing needs of people.

The majority of the sericulture farmers are small and marginal. It is realised that these small and marginal farmers constitute a resource base for major agricultural programmes so that increase in productivity for the small and marginal farmers can provide significant boost to the national economic growth as well as improved income distribution within the country. Among other countries, China has gone ahead with the maximum utilization of the land for increasing the economic growth.

It is observed that studies with regard to farmers allocative efficiency and subsequent increase in productivity have been carried substantially on cereals and pulses. However, specific studies have not been carried out in the Mulberry cultivation and cocoon rearing with a view to understand the education or allocative efficiency in production process. Mulberry cultivation is also similar to agricultural operations being simple and easy, on the other hand silkworm rearing is a quite complicated process, requiring specific management skills with due understanding of their various technical aspects involved therein. The acquired capabilities of farm people are of primary importance in sericulture. The acquired capabilities are neither inborn nor provided at any age of life, and to acquire such capabilities one has to pay the price. This is in essence, an investment in human capital.

To cope up with the changing aspects of transfer of technology and efficent use of inputs in sericulture, education and training are necessary to boost the level of productivity. In this context, education in a situation of *long run equilibrium in traditional agriculture* would be of very little economic value to *small utility maximizing farmers*, but would be an *important economic input for sericulture farmers* who are largely participating in the market oriented produce.

The main aim of this study is to examine the precise relationship between education and its impact on management, productivity (economic variables) and the other aspects like modernization in values and beliefs, social mobility, social relations, and decision making process etc., (Non-economic Variables) on the sericulture farmers. The present study entitled "*Education and Development—A Study of Human Capital Formation*" is based on the primary data collected from the farmers of two villages in Hindupur Mandal in Ananthapur district of Andhra Pradesh. The variables included in this study are:

1. Level of schooling;
2. Exposure to different literature relating to sericulture;
3. Productivity of farmers;
4. Exposure to different methods of rearing;
5. Income; and
6. Attitudes towards social life.

Objectives

The present study has been designed and carried out with the following objectives:

1. To study the impact of education on socio-economic development of sericulture farmers;
2. To analyse the relationship between levels of education and productivity among sericulture farmers;
3. To study the role of education in offering appropriate knowledge for farmers in changing, modernizing environment; and
4. To assess the impact of education on social issues like values, attitudes and modernity.

Methodology

The research methodology employed in this study is survey method. Structured schedules were administered to selected respondents in the study area. Before launching of main study, the interview schedules were pre-tested.

Consequent upon modifications therein, the principal survey was undertaken. Based on the śecondary data available at Directorate of Sericulture, Hyderabad, Anantapur district was selected for the study. The criteria followed in selecting the district were the existance of highest number of sericulture farmers and higher acrage under mulberry cultivation.

To delineate the differences of social, economic, political and attitudinal aspects among the farmers, one (Maluguru) village was selected where all farmers had adopted sericulture as their primary occupation. The second village (Tumakunta) was selected purposively where many respondents had not adopted sericulture as their primary occupation.

In the village (Maluguru) where predominantly sericulture cultivators are staying the respondents were selected and interviewed as per the list provided by the Assistant Director (Hindupur Circle), sericulture. In the second village, (Tumakunta) the respondents were selected from the voters list supplied by the village surpanch. The whole analysis is based on the farmers formal educational level and its subsequent impact on managerial skills, productivity, population quality etc.

References

1. *Indian Constitution - Government of India*, New Delhi, 1950.
2. Education and National Development - *The Report of Education Commission 1964 - 66*, Government of India, New Delhi.
3. Coombes, Philip H, Roy prosser and Manzoor Ahmed - *New paths to Learning for Rural Children and Youth*, UNICEF, International Council for Educational Development, New York, 1973.
4. Chaudhri, D.P. - *Education and Agricutlural Productivity in India*, Ph.D Thesis, University of Delhi, Delhi, 1968.
5. Schumpeter, J.A. - *History of Economic Analysis* New York, 1954.
6. Warren C.Baum - *Investing in Development: Lessons of World Bank Experience*, World bank, Oxford University Press, New York, 1985.
7. World Bank - *Education Sector Policy paper*, Washington D.C, 1980.
8. Lockheed, Marlaine E, John Middleton and Greeta Nettleton - "Educational Technology: Sustainable and Effective use" in Education and Employment,Background Paper PHREE/91/32, *World Bank*, population and Human Resources Development, Washington D.C, 1991.
9. ——————"Educational Technology: Sustainable and Effective use" in Education and Employment Background paper, *World Bank*, Washington D.C, 1991.
10. Schultz, T.W. - *Transforming Traditional Agriculture*, New Heaven, Yale University Press, London, 1964.
11. ——————, "Investment in Human Capital" in *Economics of Education* (Eds.) M.Blaug Vol.I, English Language Book Society and Penguin Books, 1968.
12. ——————, "Capital Formation by Education", *Journal of political Economy*, December, 1960.
13. ——————, *The Economics of Being Poor*, Nobel Lecture, Nobel Foundation, Stockholm, 1979.

14. Mellor, John.W - *The Economics of Agricultural Development*, Cornell University Press, Ithacca, 1966.

15. Rostow, W.W - *The stages of Economic Growth*,Cambridge University Press, Cambridge, 1960.

16. Marshall, A - *The Principles of Economics*, Mac Millian, Book IV, 1890.

17. Dobb, M - *Some Aspects of Economic Development*, Delhi School of Economics, Delhi, 1957.

18. Arthur Lewis, W - *The Theory of Economic Growth*, Richard D.Irrwin, Inc. Homewood, Illinois, U.S.A, 1955.

19. Inkeles, Alex and Smith David - *Becoming Modern : Individual change in Six Developing Countries*, Massachusetts, Harvard University Press, London, 1974.

20. Denison, Edward. F - *Why Growth Rates Differ*? The Brookings Institution, Washington D.C., 1967.

21. Bowman, M.J. et.al - *Readings in the Economics of Education, (Eds.)* UNESCO, Paris, 1968.

22. Strumilin, S.G. - The Economic significance of people's Education", cited in Huq, M.S, *Education, Manpower and Development in South and South-East Asia, 1924.*

23. Alva, Myrdal - "The power of Education", in *Education in World perspective (Eds.)* by Emmet John Hughes, Lancer Books, New York, 1965.

24. Nalla Goundan, A.M - *Education and Development: A study of Human Capital Formation and its Role in Economic Development in India*, Ph.D Thesis, Kurukshetra University, Kurukshetra, 1965.

25. World Bank - *World Development Report*, World Bank, Washington D.C., 1980.

26. Government of India - *The First Five Year Plan 1951 - 56*, Planning Commission, New Delhi, 1952.

27. Government of India - *The Seventh Five year Plan 1980 - 85*, Vol.

I, Planning Commission, New Delhi, 1985.

28. ————, *The Seventh Five Year Plan 1980 - 85*, Vol.I, Planning Commission, New Delhi, 1985.

29. Lockheed, Marlaine E., Dean T. Jamison and Lawrance Lau - "Farmer Education and Farm Efficiency: A survey", *Journal of Economic Development and Cultural Change, 29/1, October, 1980.*

30. Schultz, T.W. - *Transforming Traditional Agriculture*, New Heaven, Yale University Press, London 1964.

31. Wharton Jr, C.R. - "Education and Agricultural Growth: The Role of Education in Early State Agriculture", cited in Anderson, C.A and Bowman, M.J. (Eds), *Education and Economic Development*, Aldine Press, Chicago, 1965.

32. Welch, F - "Education and Production", *Journal of Political Economy*, Vol.78, No.1, Jan - Feb, 1970.

33. Bowman, M.J - "Concerning the Role of Education", cited in the *Human Investment in Economic Thought* (Eds) by Mark Blaug, 1976.

34. Lockheed, et.al - "Farmer Education and Farm Efficiency : A Survey", *Journal of Economic Development and Cultural Change*, 29/1 October, 1980.

35. Chaudhari, D.P - "Education in Production and Modernizing Agriculture in Asian underdeveloped countries - Structural Re-Adjustment in *Asian perspective*, Vol.I, Centre paper, No.17, Japan Economic Research Centre, Tokyo, 1971.

36. Cotlear, Daniel - "Farmer Education and Farm Efficiency in Peru: The role of Schooling, Extension Services and Migration", EDT Discussion paper 49, *World Bank*, population and Human Resource Development, Washington D.C, 1986.

37. Eisemon, Thomas. O; John Schwille and Robert Prouty - Empirical Results and Conventional Wisdom, "Strategies for increasing Primary School Effectiveness in Burundi", *Mimeo*, 1989.

38. Adamski, I - "Improved Peasant Farming as a Result of the Social and Professional Activities of the Farmers", *International Jour-*

nal of Agrarian Affairs, Vol.V, No.4, July, 1969.

39. Harker, Bruce Rogers - *Education Communication and Agricultural Changes - A Study of Japanese Farmers*, Unpunished Ph.D Thesis, University of Chicago, 1971.

40. Rati Ram—"Role of Education in Production: A Slightly New Approach", *Quarterly Journal of Economics*, Vol.95, No.2, September, 1980.

41. Som P.Pudasaini - "The Effects of Education in Agriculture: Evidence from Nepal". *American Journal of Agricultural Economics*, Vol.65, No.3, August, 1983.

42. Gisser, M - Schooling and the Farm Problem,*Econometrica*, Vol.33, No.3, July, 1965.

43. Venkatasubramanian, K - "Education and Economic Development in India", cited in Tilak Jandhyala B.G, Returns to Education in India: A Review, *Bulletin of Indian Institute of Education*, Pune, Vol.II, 1981.

44. Jamison, D.T. and Lau, L.J - *Farmer Education and Farm Efficiency*, Washington D.C, 1978.

45. Kothari, Rajani - Education and National Development, *Report of the Education Commission*, Government of India, New Delhi, 1964.

46. Majumdar, Vina - *Education and Social Change*, Indian Institute of Advanced Study, Shimla, 1972.

47. Bhatia, S.C and Gupta, N.P. - *Linking Literacy with Development* (Eds), Indian Adult Association, New Delhi, 1980.

48. Rudolph, S.M and Rudolph, L.I - *Education and Politics in India: Studies in Organization, Society and Polity* (Eds), Oxford University Press, New Delhi, 1972.

49. Inkeles, A and Smith, D.H - *Becoming Modern : Individual Change in Six Developing Countries*, Massachusetts, Harvard University Press, Cambridge, 1974.

50. Singh, A.K - *Differential Impact of Education, Industrialization and Urbanization on Modernity*, Center for International Af-

fairs, Harvard University Press, Cambridge, 1968.

51. Singh, S.N - *Industrialization in Modern Perspective*, Classical Publications, New Delhi, 1979.

52. *Inkeles and David H.Smith - Becoming Modern : Individual Change in Six Developing Countries*, Massachusetts, Harvard University Press, Cambridge, 1974.

53. *UNICEF* - Assignment Children, No.49/50, Geneva, Spring, 1980.

54. UNO—*Poverty, Unemployment and Development Policy: A Case Study of Selected Issues with reference to Kerala*, New York, 1975.

55. Christopher, Colclough—"Primary Schooling and Economic Development : A Review of Evidence" World Bank Staff Working Paper, *World Bank*, Washington D.C, 1980.

56. Gopinadhan Nair, P.R.—*Primary Education, Population Growth and Socio-Economic Change: A Comparative Study with Particular Reference to Kerala*, Allied Publishers, New Delhi, 1981.

57. Panikar, P.G.K—"Resources Not the Constraint on Health Improvement: A Case Study of Kerala", in the *Economic and Political Weekly*, Vol.XIV, No.44, November, 1979.

58. Operational Research Group—*Family Planning Practices in India.* The Fifth All India Survey Report, Baroda, 1979.

2

PROFILE OF STUDY AREA AND RESPONDENTS

"Education is the manifestation of perception already present in man".

— Swamy Vivekananda

With a view to understand the impact of Formal Education on Sericulture Farmers, an empirical study was carried out in Maluguru and Tumakunta Villages of Hindupur Mandal of Anantapur District in Andhra Pradesh.

The Anantapur District derives its name from its headquarters town. Anantapur District is neither a geographical, historical nor an ethnical entity but is the creation for administrative convenience.

Geographical Features

Location

Anantapur District is situated in the western most part of Deccan Plateau and forms the southrern most part of the Rayalaseema Region of Andhra Pradesh. Its geographical area is 19134 sq kms and is situated within 13° - 41' and 15° - 14' N and 76° - 47' and 78° - 26'E. It is bounded on the north by Kurnool district, on the east by Cuddapah and on the south and West by Karnataka State.

Climate

The year may be divided into four seasons. The period from December to February is the dry and comparatively cool season. The summer season is from March to May and is followed by the south-west monsoon season from June to September. Being far away from the east-coast it does not enjoy the full benefit of the north -eastern monsoon and being cut off by the high western ghats, the south - west monsoon is also prevented. Due to its unfortunate situation this district is deprived of both the monsoons. October and November form the retreating monsoon season.

Rainfall

The average annual rainfall in the district is 546 mm. The rainfall generally increases from the north-west to the south-east. The rainfall in the district is chiefly confined to the months of May to November, the highest rainfall is usually recorded in the month of September.

Land-use Pattern

During the last decade 1980 - 81 to 1990 - 91 the net sown area has increased to 53%. Mulberry plantations were started around 1970's and picked up by 1975. Later this was spread into other districts of the region. By 1991 about 80,500 hectares was brought under Mulberry Plantations. The area under Mulberry Plantation in Anantapur district is 31,139 hectares (1991).

Demographic Features

The district has a population of 25.48 lakhs as per 1981 census accounting for 4.8% of the states population. The growth rate for the past two decennial periods are 19.7% and 20.4% respectively indicating lower growth rate when compared to the state average of 23.19%. The density of population is 133 per sq.km in the district against 195 per sq. km of the State. The literate population constitutes 29% of the total population compared to state average of 30%. 79% of the population live in villages. Scheduled Caste population constitute about 14%, Scheduled Tribe about 3% and minority community about 12%. The work force in the district constitutes about 42% of the total population. There are 946 females per 1000 males.

Profile of the Respondents

In this chapter an attempt has been made to present the profile of 220 respondents, analysing their socio-economic parameters selected from Maluguru and Tumakunta villages of Hindupur mandal of Anantapur district. The basic variables studied are religion, educational status, occupational patterns (Primary as well as secondary), number of layings reared per crop, annual income, knowledge about the Mulberry plantation and knowledge about the different aspects of cocoon rearing. The respondents are categorised as cultivators and non-cultivators. The cultivator category is largely drawn from the Maluguru village whereas the non- cultivator category is drawn from Tumukunta village in the study region. Of these respondents, 170 were mulberry cultivators as well as cocoon rears belonging to Maluguru and among remaining 50 respondents, 32 are non-cultivators and 18 are cultivators belonging to Tumakunta village. The break up of the respondents by Mandal and village-wise is shown in Table 2.1.

Table 2.1 : Distribution of Respondents by Mandal and Village-wise

Sl. No.	*Name of the District*	*Name of the Mandal*	*Name of the Village*	*No. of Respondents*
1.	Anantapur	Hindupur	Maluguru	170
2.	Anantapur	Hindupur	Tumakunta	50
	Total			**220**

Social-Composition of Respondents

Religion

It may be seen from Table 2.2 that 97% of the respondents professing Hindu religion and 3% of the respondents professing Muslim religion. The data reveal that the existence of Hindu cultivators is more than Muslim cultivators.

Caste Composition

An attempt has been made in the selected villages to know the extent and number of different castes engaged in sericulture. It may be seen from the Table 2.3 and Graph 2.1 that 30% of respondents belonged to Scheduled Castes Community, 0.9% to Scheduled Tribe community, 55.0% to

Table 2.2 : Distribution of Respondents by Religious Status

		Name of the Villages		
Sl.No.	*Religion*	*Maluguru*	*Tumakunta*	*Total*
1.	Hindu	166 (97.65)	47 (94.0)	213 (96.82)
2.	Muslim	4 (2.35)	3 (6.0)	7 (3.18)
	Total	**170** **(100.0)**	**50** **(100.0)**	**220** **(100.0)**

(Figures in Parenthesis indicate percentages)

Table 2.3 : Different Social Groups Among Respondents

		Social Groups				
Sl.No.	*Name of the Village*	SC	ST	OBC	OC	*Total*
1.	Maluguru	46	--	95	29	170 (77.27)
2.	Tumakunta	20	2	26	2	50 (22.73)
	Total	**66** **(30.0)**	**2** **(0.9)**	**121** **(55.0)**	**31** **(14.1)**	**220** **(100.0)**

(Figures in Parenthesis indicate percentages)

backward classes and 14.1% respondents belonged to other castes. Table-2.4 further reveal that among the Scheduled Castes, Madiga community accounted for 25.91% and among backward classes Kuraba and Boya castes accounted for 23.18% and 20.45% respectively.

Educational status

Education is one of the important components for the development of any society. The operational definition of 'education' used here conveys the concept of formal education. The distribution of respondents by different levels of education is presented in Table 2.5 and in Graph 2.2.

The Table 2.5 revealed that 27% of the respondents from Maluguru were illiterate whereas in Tumakunta 52% of respondents were found illiterate. By and large, educational level is higher among Maluguru respondents than Tumakunta respondents.

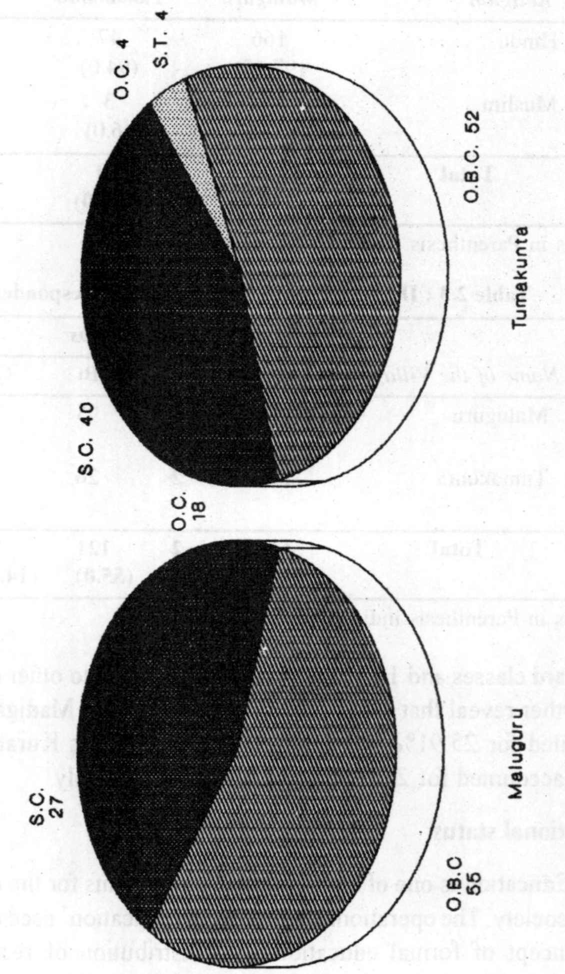

Graph 2.1 : Caste-wise Break-up of the Respondents

Table 2.4 : Caste-wise Break-up of the Respondents

(No. of Respondents)

		Selected Villages		
Sl.No.	*Name of the Caste*	*Maluguru*	*Tumakunta*	*Total*
1.	Madiga (SC)	40 (23.5)	17 (34.0)	57 (25.9)
2.	Mala (SC)	6 (3.5)	3 (6.0)	9 (4.1)
3.	Muslim (OBC)	4 (2.4)	3 (6.0)	7 (3.2)
4.	Reddy (OC)	18 (10.6)	2 (4.0)	20 (9.1)
5.	Brahmin (OC)	2 (1.8)	---	2 (0.9)
6.	Lingayat (OBC)	1 (0.6)	---	1 (0.5)
7.	Vishya (OC)	7 (4.1)	---	7 (3.2)
8.	Jain (OC)	2 (1.8)	---	2 (0.9)
9.	Kuruba (OBC)	35 (20.6)	16 (32.0)	51 (23.2)
10.	Boya (OBC)	40 (23.5)	5 (10.0)	45 (20.5)
11.	Chakali (OBC)	1 (0.6)	---	1 (0.5)
12.	Balija (OBC)	9 (5.3)	1 (2.0)	10 (4.5)
13.	Gouda (OBC)	3 (1.8)	---	3 (1.4)
14.	Golla (OBC)	2 (1.2)	1 (2.0)	3 (1.4)
15.	Valmiki (ST)	---	2 (4.0)	2 (0.9)
	Total	**170** **(100.0)**	**50** **(100.0)**	**220** **(100.0)**

(Figures in Parenthesis indicate percentages)

Table 2.5 : Distribution of Respondents by Educational Status

Sl.No.	Educational Levels	Selected Villages		Total
		Maluguru	Tumakunta	
1.	Illiterates	46 (27.1)	26 (52.0)	72 (32.7)
2.	Primary	62 (36.5)	12 (24.0)	74 (33.6)
3.	Middle	29 (17.1)	7 (14.0)	36 (16.4)
4.	Secondary	23 (13.5)	4 (8.0)	27 (12.3)
5.	Higher Secondary	10 (5.9)	1 (2.0)	11 (5.0)
	Total	**170 (100.0)**	**50 (100.0)**	**220 (100.0)**

(Figures in Parenthesis indicate percentages)

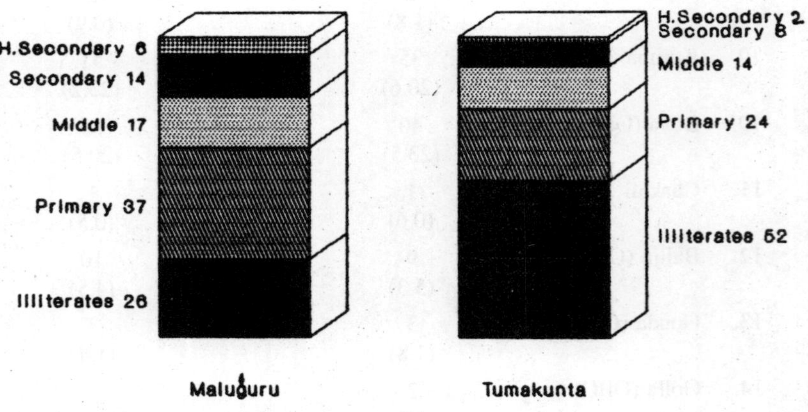

Graph 2.2 : Distribution of Respondents by Educational Status

Marital Status

For the purpose of eliciting information with regard to marital status, specific question was introduced in the interview schedule. The response may be seen in Table 2.6 where 87.65% among the respondents belonging to Maluguru village were married, whereas 96% respondents belonging to Tumakunta were married. The percentage of unmarried respondents of Maluguru was higher than the percentage of Tumakunta respondents. While selecting the respondents among sericulture cultivators within the household, I,interviewed the person who was actually engaged in sericulture rather than traditional way of selecting head of the household for interviewing. This norm has created the higher percentage of unmarried respondents among cultivators.

Table 2.6 : Distribution of Respondents by Marital Status

Sl.No.	*Educational Levels*	*Selected Villages*		*Total*
		Maluguru	*Tumakunta*	
1.	Married	149 (87.65)	48 (96.0)	197 (89.55)
2.	Unmarried	21 (12.35)	2 (4.0)	23 (10.45)
	Total	**170 (100.0)**	**50 (100.0)**	**220 (100.0)**

(Figures in Parenthesis indicate percentages)

Occupational Distribution

The distribution of respondents according to the primary occupation is given in Table 2.7.

It may be seen from Table 2.7 that all the respondents belonging to Maluguru were engaged in sericulture cultivation. In Tumakunta village, 36% of respondents are having sericulture as their primary occupation. But the percentage of agricultural labourers among respondents in Tumakunta village was as high as 50 percent, whereas in Maluguru village none were having agricultural labour as their main occupation. One of the reasons for less population of Agricultural Labourers is due to the concentration of mulberry cultivation and cocoon rearing.

Table 2.7 : Distribution of Respondents by Primary Occupation

Sl.No.	*Educational Levels*	*Selected Villages*		*Total*
		Maluguru	*Tumakunta*	
1.	Sericulture (Mulberry + Cocoon rearing)	170 (100.00)	18 (36.0)	188 (85.45)
2.	Agriculture	---	2 (4.0)	2 (0.91)
3.	Agri. Labour	---	25 (50.0)	25 (11.36)
4.	Factory work	---	5 (10.0)	5 (2.27)
	Total	**170 (100.0)**	**50 (100.0)**	**220 (100.0)**

(Figures in Parenthesis indicate percentages)

Land Holding Pattern

Land is one of the important resources on which one can sustain, and at the same time it is pre-requisite for mulberry cultivation. There are farmers who rear silkworms by purchase of mulberry leaf from the neighbouring farmers. The percentage of this type of farmers is very less. However, farmers prefers to have the land right, though fragmented within the vicinity of village. There are two different types of land on which different crops analysed in the study (i) Lands which are used for exclusively mulberry cultivation and (ii) lands which are used for cereals/pulses production.

As regards the land holding pattern and variety of seedlings owned by respondents interms of rainfed, irrigated, local and improved, it was found that majority of the farmers are having dry land but the extent of irrigated land was more than unirrigated land as far as sericulture is concerned. The Table 2.8 presents the mulberry cultivator's land holding pattern.

There are two types of mulberry gardens existing in this area. They are local and improved varieties cultivated under rainfed and irrigated conditions. Considering these important variables the respondents have been categorised into three groups (i) those farmers who are cultivating

Table 2.8 : Land Holding Pattern among the Respondents (Mulberry)

Sl. No.	Types of Land & Variety of Mulberry	No. of Farmers and Extent of Land		
		Maluguru	Tumakunta	Total
1.	No. of Farmers	102 (60.0)	7 (14.0)	109 (49.54)
2.	Area under cultivation (Rainfed Local)	75.48 (31.78)	6.00 (36.4)	81.48 (32.08)
3.	No. of Farmers	63 (37.0)	10 (20.0)	73 (33.18)
4.	Area under cultivation (Irrigated + Local)	129.60 (54.56)	9.45 (57.4)	139.05 (54.75)
5.	No. of Farmers	5 (3.0)	1 (2.0)	6 (2.72)
6.	Area under cultivation (Irrigated + Improved)	32.44 (13.6)	1.00 (6.1)	33.44 (13.16)
7.	Non-cultivators	---	32 (64.0)	32 (14.55)
	Total	**170 (100.0)**	**50 (100.0)**	**220 (100.0)**
	Total Land	**237.52 (100.0)**	**16.45 (100.0)**	**253.97 (100.0)**

(Figures in Parenthesis indicate percentages)

lands under rainfed conditon of local mulberry variety (ii) those farmers who are cultivating lands under irrigated condition of local mulberry variety and finally (iii) those farmers who are cultivating lands under irrigated condition as well improved variety of mulberry.

In Maluguru there were about 60.0% respondents who manages 75.48 acres of land under the category of rainfed condition of local mulberry variety. In the second category there were 37.0% respondents who manages 129.60 acres of land under the category of irrigated condition of local variety. In the third category there were about 3.0% respondents who manages 32.44 acres of land under the category of irrigated condition of improved variety. As such, the land per farmer on an average was found to be only 0.75 acres among the first category (Rainfed + Local) of

respondents. In other words, majority of the farmers were holding fragmented land holdings. But in the second category (Irrigated + Local) land per farmer on an average was about 2.0 acres which has got irrigation facility. In the third category (Irrigated + Improved) where land was irrigated as well as improved variety of mulberry garden was about 6.5 acres on an average. These are the farmers who can command all resources including sericulture department's attention.

In Tumakunta no distinctive difference was existing among these three categories of farmers. In all the categories average land per farmer was less than one acre or just about one acre.

Some farmers were cultivating cereals/oil seeds like groundnut, bajra , paddy and wheat etc., in their lands apart from cultivating mulberry. There were 63.0% respondents belonging to Maluguru village cultivating groundnut to the extent of 240.5 acres. In Tumakunta village 36.0% respondents are cultivating groundnut to the extent of 26 acres. And also about 40.0% and 13.5% respondents who are cultivating bajra , paddy and wheat to the extent of 52.46 and 44.28 acres respectively. Table 2.9 presents the distribution of respondents by crop-wise cultivation.

Table 2.9 : Crop-wise Distribution of Respondents (other than Mulberry)

Sl.No.	*Different crops*	*Selected Villages*		
		Maluguru Number & extent	*Tumakunta Number & extent*	*Total Number & extent*
1.	No. of farmers	107	18	125
	Ground nut (Ac)	240.5	26	266.5
2.	No. of farmers	68	18	86
	Ragi (Ac)	52.46	12.51	64.97
3.	No. of farmers	23	11	34
	Paddy & Wheat (Ac)	44.28	15.15	59.43
4.	Non-cultivators	---	32	32
Total Number of Farmers &		**170**	**18**	**188**
Total Extent of Land		**337.24**	**53.66**	**390.0**

(Figures in Parenthesis indicate percentages)

Some farmers were depending on cereals/oil seed crops apart from the earnings which they got from mulberry cultivation. Enquired about the utilization of land other than the mulberry, cereals and oil seed crops revealed that the farmers raise crops other than mulberry because of obvious reason. Had there been any little chance, they could have cultivated mulberry in these lands also. But the area under different crops is very less. The available data are presented in Table 2.10.

Table 2.10 : Distribution of Respondents into Other Crops

Sl.No.	*Educational Levels*	*Selected Villages*		*Total*
		Maluguru	*Tumakunta*	
1.	No. of Farmers	2	2	4
2.	Area under Red chillies	4.75	1.0	5.75
3.	No. of farmers	3	3	6
4.	Area under sugar cane	8.50	5.50	14.0
Total No. of Farmers &		**5**	**5**	**10**
Total Extent of Land		**13.25**	**6.50**	**19.75**

(Figures in Parenthesis indicate percentages)

Those farmers who were cultivating sugarcane as well as mulberry had large extent of own lands. They not only control sufficient land but also access to sufficient water to go for this type of crops.

The respondents were classified into different groups based on the extent of the land (exclusively Mulberry) they are possessing, (Table 2.11) it is revealed that there were 55.9% and 14.0% respondents having less than 1 ac, 37.6% and 22.0% respondents having less than 2.00 Ac, 1.2% and nil respondents were having less than 5.0 Ac and 5.3% and nil respondents were having 10.0 Ac in the villages of Maluguru and Tumakunta respectively. Since Tumakunta village was selected purposively to delineate the differences of socio-economic, and attitudinal aspects, the existence of marginal cultivators and landless respondents (64.0%) are note worthy. In the villages under study, those who are having more than 2 acres of Mulberry garden are treated as big and respected farmers.

Cropping Pattern

The cropping pattern prevalent in both the villages comprise sug-

Table 2.11 : Distribution of Respondents Based on the Extent of Land (Exclusively Mulburry Gardens)

Sl. No.	Extent of land holding	Selected Villages: Maluguru	Tumakunta	Total
1.	Less than 1 Ac	95 (55.9)	7 (14.0)	102 (46.4)
2.	1.1 Ac to 2.00 Ac	64 (37.6)	11 (22.0)	75 (34.1)
3.	2.1 Ac to 5.00 Ac	2 (1.2)	---	2 (0.90)
4.	5.1 Ac to 10.00 Ac	9 (5.3)	---	9 (4.1)
5.	Landless	---	32 (64.0)	32 (14.1)
	Total	**170 (100.0)**	**50 (100.0)**	**220 (100.0)**

(Figures in Parenthesis indicate percentages)

arcane, groundnut etc., apart from Mulberry. Those respondents who were having more land could grow Mulberry as well as other crops. But those who were having small piece of land could grow only one type of crop. There is a big pond adjacent to Maluguru village which can be called as a natural gift to the Mulberry cultivators. In rainy season the tank gets filled with water and this can be used as and when the farmers need water. Sometimes mansoon may not set in time or may fail. To cope up this situation, those farmers who are well off have gone in for borewell/ tubewells. The big farmers who are having large extent of mulberry garden divide the land and feed silkworms as per requirement. In this process, they can rear one batch in every month. In this rotation the farmer is always busy and the process of growing Mulberry garden and rearing cocoons goes on through out the year.

Number of Crops in a Year

In Mulberry cultivation a farmer can take two to three crops even in dry lands. If irrigation is assured, a farmer can take even 5 to 6 crops in a year. In this process even if one crop fails, the farmer will not be in loss. Only those farmers who are going for 2 - 3 crops, if they fail in one crop, the farmers will be in great loss. The frequency of number of crops taken up by respondents in a year can be seen in Table 2.12 and in Graph 3.

Table 2.12 : Distribution of Respondents and their Frequency of Crops in a Year

Sl.No.	*No. of Crops*	*Selected Villages*		*Total*
		Maluguru	*Tumakunta*	
1.	1 crop	1 (1.2)	---	2 (0.90)
2.	2 crops	31 (18.2)	2 (4.0)	33 (15.0)
3.	3 crops	60 (35.3)	6 (12.0)	66 (30.0)
4.	4 crops	65 (38.2)	7 (14.0)	72 (32.72)
5.	5 crops	3 (1.8)	3 (6.0)	6 (8.72)
6.	6 & more crops	9 (5.3)	---	9 (4.09)
7.	Non-cultivators	---	32 (64.)	32 (14.54)
	Total	**170** **(100.0)**	**50** **(100.0)**	**220** **(100.0)**

(Figures in Parenthesis indicate percentages)

It can be seen from above Table that about 54.7 per cent of Maluguru farmers were taking from one to three crops in a year. But in Tumakunta only 16 per cent of farmers were taking one to three crops. About 40 per cent of the cultivators from Maluguru were taking 4–5 crops in a year, whereas 20 per cent of the respondents from Tumakunta were falling under this category. Only 5.3 per cent of the respondents from Maluguru were taking 6 and more crops but none in Tumakunta. This indicates that taking 6 and more crops in a year is only possible for to big farmers, and those who can command other resources.

Disease Free Layings (DFLs) Per Crop

While examining the number of crops taken up in a year, information

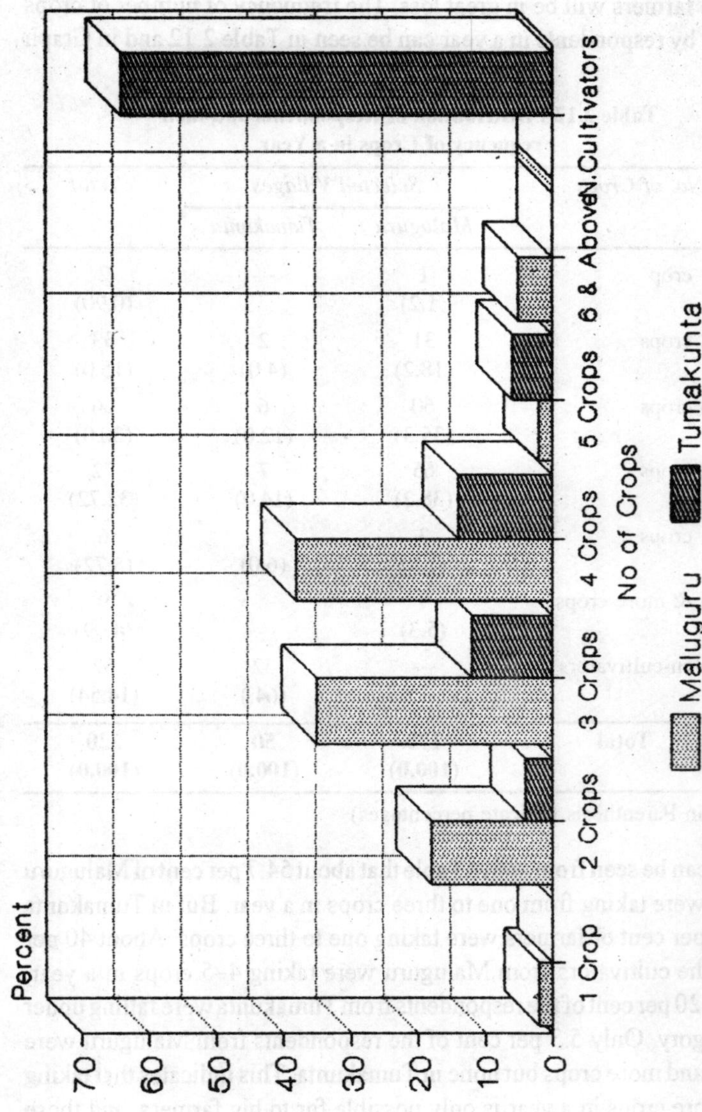

Graph 2.3 : Distribution of Respondents on the Frequency of Crops in a Year

was also collected in regard to how many DFLs were reared per crop. The Table 2.13 presents the details.

Table 2.13 : Distribution of Respondents and DFLs per Crop

Sl.No.	*No. of DFL's*	*Selected Villages*		*Total*
		Maluguru	*Tumakunta*	
1.	100–200	141 (82.94)	14 (28.0)	155 (70.45)
2.	201–400	12 (7.06)	4 (8.0)	16 (7.27)
3.	401–600	9 (5.29)	---	9 (4.09)
4.	601–1000	6 (3.53)	---	6 (2.73)
5.	1001 & above	2 (1.18)	---	2 (0.91)
6.	Non-cultivators	---	32 (64.0)	32 (14.55)
	Total	**170** **(100.0)**	**50** **(100.0)**	**220** **(100.0)**

(Figures in Parenthesis indicate percentages)

Among the respondents 82.94% belonging to Maluguru were rearing between 100–200 DFLs per crop. This indicates that rearing more than 200 DFLs needs lot of managerial capabilities and sufficient mulberry garden. 77% respondents of Tumakunta, were found rearing in the same range. There were about 12.35% and 3.53% respondents who were rearing 201–600 and 801–1000 DFLs respectively at Maluguru. Only 2 respondents, whose percentage was 1.18 were rearing 1001 and above in Maluguru. The area of land, financial feasibility and other infrastructural facilities are important inputs required for rearing more number of DFLs. For majority of the respondents it is possible only to rear 100–200 DFLs.

Place of rearing

Place of rearing is one of the important pre-requisites for rearing silkworms. There are so many specifications and manners while constructing a rearing house. The temperature, ventilation and humidity is controlled through the windows of a rearing house. Since this is one of the important infrastructure through which one can increase his productivity, and thereby better income accumulation. Table 2.14 given below describes the type of facility the respondents were having with regard to the place of rearing.

Table 2.14 : Distribution of Respondents and Place of Rearing Silkworms

Sl.No.	Place of rearing	Selected Villages		Total
		Maluguru	Tumakunta	
1.	Own shed	44 (25.9)	2 (4.0)	46 (20.9)
2.	Within the House	90 (52.9)	15 (30.0)	105 (47.7)
3.	Rented Shed	36 (21.2)	1 (2.0)	37 (16.8)
4.	Non-cultivators	---	32 (64.0)	32 (18.8)
	Total	**170 (100.0)**	**50 (100.0)**	**220 (100.0)**

(Figures in Parenthesis indicate percentages)

There were about 25.9% respondents who were having their own rearing shed, and about 52.9% respondents were rearing within their house and about 21.2% respondents were rearing in rented sheds at Maluguru. The same pattern was found in Tumakunta as 4.0%, 20.0% and 2.0% were rearing in own shed, within the house and rented sheds respectively. In both the villages, highest number of farmers were rearing within their house. Rearing within the house needs lot of protective measures which many of the respondents did not adhere. Under some strong reasons, namely may not afford to pay the rent and sometimes sheds may not be available on rent at that particular time. Those who were having their own shed have had advantage in rearing silkworms. As soon as mulbery leaf gets ready, immediatly rearing house has got to be disinfected and attend to other petty works. The problem with rented shed is that if the previous person, due to lack of knowledge could not disinfect properly, there is a possibility of disease spread which may reoccur if the new incumbent did not attend properly.

Livestock Position

In a village situation, it is common to have few animals in their premises. Some people may rear buffaloes or cows to derive income in addition to their primary income. Some farmers keep bullocks and other kinds of animals to cultivate, their lands as well as mulberry gardens. Information was collected to know the number and what type of animals that the respondents were keeping. The Table 2.15 presents the picture.

Table 2.15 : Distribution of Respondents on Livestock Position

Sl.No.	*Livestock*	*Selected Villages*					
		Maluguru		*Tumakunta*		Total	
		No. of ani-mals	No. of far-mers	No. of ani-mals	No. of far-mers	No. of ani-mals	No. of far-mers
1.	Cows	148 (31.36)	64 (37.6)	20 (13.51)	14 (28.0)	168 (27.10)	78 (35.45)
2.	Buffaloes	65 (13.77)	34 (20.0)	11 (7.43)	6 (12.)	76 (12.25)	40 (18.18)
3.	Bullocks	93 (19.70)	33 (19.41)	17 (11.49)	8 (16.0)	110 (17.74)	41 (18.64)
4.	Goat/Sheeps	41 (8.69)	7 (4.12)	76 (51.35)	8 (16 .0)	117 (18.87)	15 (6.82)
5.	Poultry	125 (26.48)	32 (18.82)	24 (16.22)	14 (28.0)	149 (24.03)	46 (20.91)
	Total	**472** **(100.0)**	**170** **(100.0)**	**148** **(100.0)**	**50** **(100.0)**	**620** **(100.0)**	**220** **(100.0)**

(Figures in Parenthesis indicate percentages)

It is evident from the Table that in both the villages more number of people were possessing cows. There were 64 respondents possessing 148 cows in Maluguru and 14 respondents possessing 20 cows in Tumakunta. In case of bullocks 33 respondents of Maluguru were in possession of 93. And in Tumakunta 8 respondents were having 17 bullokcs. For a small farmer, keeping goat / sheep comes in handy whenever he is in need of agricultural inputs. The average goat/sheep per farmer in possession was higher in Tumukunta than in Maluguru. Keeping some animal in their cattle shed is some times believed as good omen.

Respondents Income

This is one of the perceptible indicator that one has to analyse carefully. There are so many avenues by which one can get income. For the purpose of clarification the source of income has been categorised into income through sericulture, income through agriculture, income through salary, income through petty business and income through agricultural wages. For many respondents major source of income was through sericulture. For big farmers income from other sources like agriculture and animal husbandry by virtue of holding land and irrigation facilities was an additive source. Respondents income and to what extent is analysed and presented in Table 2.16 and in Graph 2.4.

There were 5.9% respondents belonging to Maluguru village whose annual income was more than one lakh from sericulture alone. This category of farmers was very few. There were 41.8% respondents whose annual income from sericulture was less than Rs. 6,000/-. And also there were 42.9% respondents whose income ranged from Rs. 6,001 to 20,000. In the next highest category there were 9.4% respondents whose annual income ranged from 20,001 to one lakh. In comparison with Maluguru, there were 10.0%, 22.0% and 4.0% respondents in Tumakunta whose income was falling under less than Rs. 6,000; 6,001 to 20,000 and 20,001 to 40,000 respectively. Remaining 64.0% respondents were not getting any income since they did not belong to farmer category.

Some farmers of both the villages were holding mulberry cultivation as well as other agricultural crops so as to increase their household income. In majority cases, income out of other agricultural crops was very less. At the same time, there were very few farmers whose agricultural income was between Rs. 60,000 to Rs. 1,00,000 annually. The Table 2.17 presented here indicate the income ranges and the distribution of respondents.

In all, 60% in Maluguru and 16.0% in Tumakunta cultivator respondents annual income from other agricultural crops was less than Rs. 1,000. This indicates that Maluguru farmers' their primary occupation was mulberry cultivation/cocoon rearing and income from other agricultural crops was of secondary importance. In additon to this, small and marginal farmers consumed domestically whatever crops (cereals) they grew in their small holdings. Around 30.0% in Maluguru and 12.0 % in Tumakunta cultivator respondents annual income had less than Rs. 6,000/-. This

Table 2.16 : Distribution of Respondents having Different Income Levels from Sericulture

Sl. No.	*Income Classification (In Rupees)*	*Selected Villages*		*Total*
		Maluguru	*Tumakunta*	
1.	Less than Rs.1,000	1 (0.59)	---	1 (0.45)
2.	Rs. 1,001 – 3,000	17 (10.0)	5 (10.0)	22 (10.0)
3.	Rs. 3,001 – 6,000	53 (31.18)	---	53 (24.09)
4.	Rs. 6,001 – 8,000	17 (10.0)	2 (4.0)	19 (8.64)
5.	Rs. 8,001 – 10,000	17 (10.0)	1 (2.0)	18 (8.18)
6.	Rs.10,001 – 15,000	24 (14.12)	3 (6.0)	27 (12.27)
7.	Rs. 15,001 – 20,000	15 (8.82)	5 (10.0)	20 (9.09)
8.	Rs. 20,001 – 40,000	9 (5.29)	2 (4.0)	11 (5.0)
9.	Rs.40,001 – 60,000	1 (0.59)	---	1 (0.45)
10.	Rs. 60,001 – 80,000	3 (1.76)	---	3 (1.36)
11.	Rs. 80,000 – 1,00,000	3 (1.76)	---	3 (1.36)
12.	Rs. 1,00,001 and above	10 (5.88)	---	10 (4.55)
13.	Non-Cultivators	---	32 (64.0)	32 (14.55)
	Total	**170 (100.0)**	**50 (100.0)**	**220 (100.0)**

(Figures in Parenthesis indicate percentages)

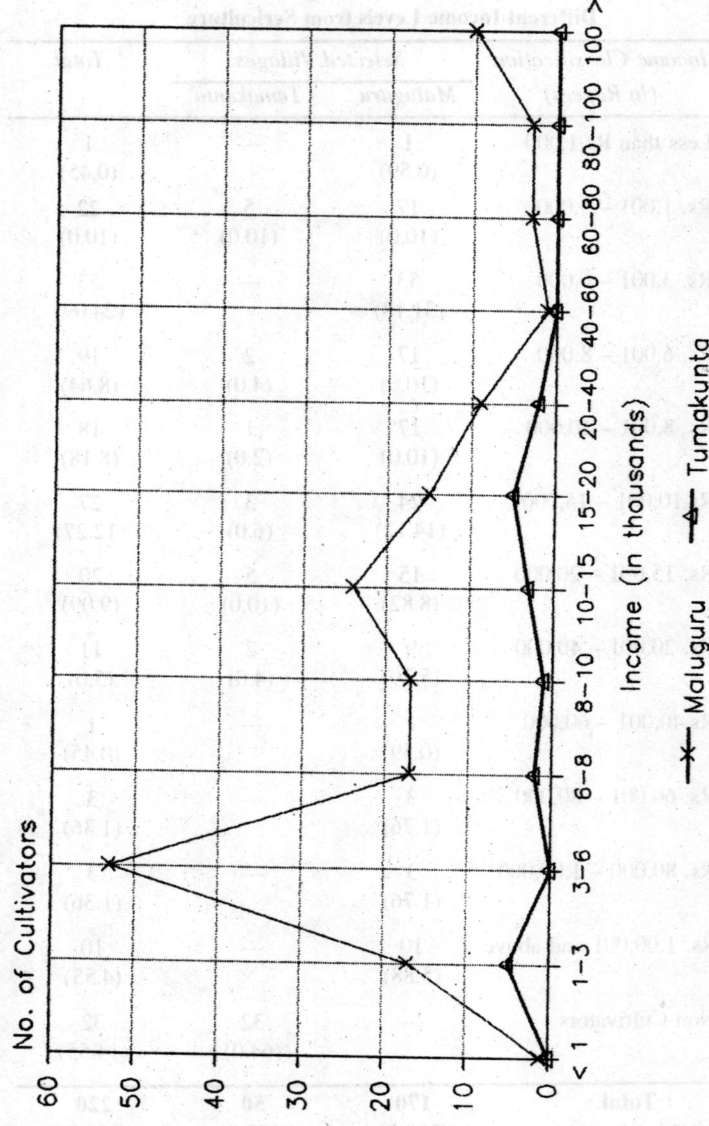

Graph 2.4 : Annual Income from Sericulture

Table 2.17 : Distribution of Respondents Income from Other Agricultural Crops

Sl. No.	*Income Classification*	*Selected Villages* Maluguru	*Selected Villages* Tumakunta	*Total*
1.	Less than Rs. 1000	102 (60.0)	8 (16.0)	142 (64.54)
2.	Rs. 1,001 to 6,000	51 (30.0)	6 (12.0)	57 (25.90)
3.	Rs. 6,001 to 20,000	8 (4.7)	2 (4.0)	10 (4.54)
4.	Rs. 20,001 to 60,000	6 (3.5)	2 (4.0)	8 (3.63)
5.	Rs. 60,001 to 1,00,000	3 (1.8)	---	3 (1.36)
6.	Non-cultivators	---	32 (64.0)	32 (14.54)
	Total	**170 (100.0)**	**50 (100.0)**	**220 (100.0)**

(Figures in Parenthesis indicate percentages)

agricultural income was substantial to medium and large farmers rather than small and marginal farmers.

When there are more number of members in the household, income from sericulture or income from other agricultural crops may not be sufficient for the requirements of its members. Some members have to go for agricultural wages. This is not uncommon, particularly among weaker sections of rural India. In many households women and old people are going to agricultural wages. In Maluguru, though respondents main occupation was mulberry, there exists agriculture labourers also. The Table 2.18 given here dipicts the income position through agricultural wages of the two villages.

There are about 47.7% respondents from Maluguru village revealed that from their households nobody was sent for agricultural wages as no requirement was felt for. The other reasons may be, social restriction and non-availability of members who could be sent for agricultural labour. In Tumakunta 80% respondents revealed that they did depend on agricultural

Table 2.18 : Distribution of Respondents Through Income from Agricultural Wages

Sl. No.	*Income Classification*	*Selected Villages*		*Total*
		Maluguru	*Tumakunta*	
1.	Upto Rs. 2,500	39 (22.94)	4 (8.0)	43 (19.54)
2.	Rs. 2,501 to Rs. 5,000	44 (25.88)	21 (42.0)	65 (29.54)
3.	Rs. 5,001 to Rs. 7,500	6 (3.53)	15 (30.0)	21 (9.54)
4.	No. of Households not going for Agriculture Labour	81 (47.65)	10 (20.0)	91 (41.26)
	Total	**170 (100.0)**	**50 (100.0)**	**220 (100.0)**

(Figures in Parenthesis indicate percentages)

wages as their main occupation and income from other sources is not sufficient to sustain the family.

Basic Amenities

The data were also collected to understand the basic amenities and social services available at Maluguru and Tumakunta. For this purpose questions were specifically enquired about the type of house, bathroom, lavatory, tap connection and electricity, and whether these were available with respondents or not. The Table 2.19 will explain the gamut of services available in these villages.

It is evident from the Table 2.19 that all respondents from Maluguru village were having shelter either pucca or kutcha house. There were about 37.7%, 36.5%, 16.5% and 7.7% respondents who occupied pucca house, mud house, Janata and thatched houses repectively in Maluguru. In the same manner, 22.0%32.0%, 4.0% and 42.0% respondents occupied pucca house, mud house, janata house and thatched houses respectively in Tumakunta. The percentage of respondents at Maluguru who occupied pucca house was more than Tumakunta. When analysed, the existance of other amenities like bath room, lavotary, tap and electricity connection, it is evident that respondents of Maluguru had more amenities than of

Table 2.19 : Table showing the Availability of Basic Amenities

Sl.No.	*Amenities*		*Selected Villages*		*Total*
			Maluguru	*Tumakunta*	
I.	i) Pucca Building		67 (39.41)	8 (16.0)	75 (34.09)
	ii) Kutcha House (Mud)		62 (36.5)	16 (32.0)	78 (35.45)
	iii) Govt. Janta House		28 (16.5)	2 (4.0)	30 (13.64)
	iv) Thatched House		13 (7.6)	21 (42.0)	34 (15.45)
	v) Hut		---	3 (1.8)	3 (1.36)
II	Bath room	– Yes –	33 (19.4)	4 (8.0)	37 (16.82)
		– No –	137 (80.6)	46 (92.0)	183 (83.18)
III	Lavotary	– Yes –	9 (5.3)	---	9 (4.09)
		– No –	161 (94.7)	50 (100.0)	211 (95.91)
IV	Tap	– Yes –	11 (6.5)	---	11 (5.0)
		– No –	159 (93.5)	50 (100.0)	209 (95.0)
V	Electricity	– Yes –	102 (60.0)	13 (26.0)	115 (52.27)
		– No –	68 (40.0)	37 (74.0)	105 (47.73)

(Figures in Parenthesis indicate percentages)

Tumakunta. Because of economic affordability and income through sericulture, the respondents of the Maluguru village were enjoying these facilities.

Summing Up

The data presented in this chapter revealed that the respondents of Maluguru Village were better in all the socio-economic indicators than to the respondents of Tumakunta. Sericulture cultivation/cocoon rearing was adopted as primary occupation in Maluguru than to Tumakunta. With regard to facilities in carrying out cocoon rearing and other basic amenities and social services Maluguru occupied better position than to Tumakunta.

3

SERICULTURE INDUSTRY: AN OVERVIEW

"Education nourishes our reasoning faculties in order to allow our mind, its freedom in the world of truth, our imagination for the world which belongs to art and our sympathy for the world of human relationship".

— Rabindranath Tagore

Silk with its graceful drape, asethetic appeal, elegance and colour has been rightly considered as "queen of textiles" and has been known in Indian sub-continent since time immemorial. Over the years its importance has been increasing and demand for silk cloth is also increasing steadily. Sericulture is one of the most integrated rural industries ancillary to agriculture supporting a large number of families providing direct and indirect employment. It involves plantation of trees/shrubs to provide leaf food to the silkworms which are reared for a period of 22-25 days, reeling of silk filament from the cocoons, twisting or doubling the filament to make the yarn of required thickness and finally to weave the silk cloth.

Morus is the Latin Word for mulberry (French: muries, Italian: gelso, Japanese : Lewwa). Production of mulberry leaves on scientific lines is essential for organising sericulture on sound economic lines. It is estimated that one metric ton of mulberry leaves is necessary for the rearing of silkworms emerging from out of one Ounce of eggs, which will yield about

25 to 30 kg of cocoons of international standard. One hectare of fertile land can produce about 15—40 tons of mulberry leaves over a twelve month period. While mulberry leaf is available for rearing in Japan, the Republic of Korea and the USSR for two to three rearing seasons a year, in the tropical countries like India, the leaves are harvested and utilised for silkworm rearing throughout the year.

Silk is produced by silkworms through secretion of silk substance known as "Fibroin" covered with sericin a gummy substance and when comes into contact with the air gets solidified and becomes silk filament. The different types of silkworms are fed on different types of leaves and they produce different varieties of silk. Nearly 70 percent of the silk produced by a silkworm is directly derived from the proteins of the mulberry leaves. India is the only country where all the known four varieties of silk are produced.

Thus, the Mulberry silkworm (Bombyxmori) eats leaves of mulberry plant, the 'Tasar' silk is produced by silkworms (Antherea) which are fed on the leaves of Oak, Arjuna or Sal trees, Eri (Philsomia ricini or Philosomia Cynthia) silk is made by worms which eat caster leaves and Muga silk is a product of worms (Antherea assama) which are fed on the leaves of Som or Soalu trees. The most popular silk is mulberry silk for its elegance, softness, sensitive to dyes etc., and accounts for 95% of world silk production. In India Mulberry silk accounts for more than 87% of the total silk produced, followed by Tasar (8%) Eri (4%) and Moga (1%)[1].

As already noted, rearing of cocoons needs knowledge and awareness of different activities involved in it. Since it involves the practitioner's level of knowledge, education formed an integral part. To know the different intricacies brief discription is given activity-wise.

Sericulture has many special advantages viz. (*i*) *It is labour intensive.* On an average, according to one estimate, 5 to 6 persons get work throughout the year for every acre of mulberry plantation. In India about 4 million persons are employed in the sericulture activity. (*ii*) *It requires less capital*-even with small amount of say Rs.2000/- a farmer can plant the mulberry and get leaves for sale to other farmers raising the silkworms. (iii) *The farmers get continuous income.* While in cereals or other crops the harvesting is once or twice in a year, the mulberry leaves can be harvested 3-4 times under rainfed conditions and 6-7 times under irrigated condtions. (iv) *The mulberry plantation gives quick returns*. After planting, the income is available within 6 to 8 months. (v) *It is highly export oriented activity* as the silk/silk fabrics earn valuable foreign exchange. (vi) The farmer can undertake all the activities including rearing of silkworms in his own farm, alongwith his other farm activities. (vii) *The mulberry plant is drought resistant* and as such provides standby support to the farmers affected by the scanty rains. (viii) *It is also highly responsive to improved agricultural practices* and application of water, fertilisers etc. Under irrigated conditions production is almost 3 times compared to the rainfed crop.

Cultivation of Mulberry Plant

Almost 50% of the cost of producing raw silk is incurred on getting the leaf food for the worms. Mulberry belongs to the genus Morus. Morus is the Latin Word for mulberry. The plant is a perennial and has an economic life of about 15 years. It is a tropical as well as temperate plant. Though the plant is grown as a bush, tree or middling the common practice in India is to grow it as bush. The plant is allowed to reach the height of 1.5 to 1.8 metres which facilitates easy harvesting of leaves.

The plant is hardy and therefore can be grown in any types of soil but red or sandy loam soil is preferable. The pH of the soil should be around 6.5. The plant can grow well upto the altitude of 700 metres above mean sea level. It can be grown in the area with rainfall ranging from 25" to 100" under rainfed conditions. Under irrigated conditions, its annual water requirement comes around 50" to 75". Leaf size is an important character taken into consideration in selecting high yielding varieties. In India Kanva- 2 high yielding variety is considered suitable in irrigated as well as in rainfed conditions. There are many other varieties also.

Harvesting

The method of harvesting of mulberry leaves depends upon rearing practices followed by the cultivators. Under leaf picking the leaves are picked individually from the plant. One can pick up tender leaves to feed young worms and more mature leaves for worms in advance age. Under branch cutting method entire branch with leaves is cut and fed to the worms after their third moult while in some areas the whole shoot i.e., branches close to the ground level are cut. The branch cutting is advantageous. It saves on labour, leaves are utilised to the maximum extent, it helps to maintain hygienic conditions and the feed quality remains better, as the leaves are attached to the branch maintaining prolonged succulency. The leaves soon after harvesting are covered with wet gunny bags to preserve their moisture and succulency generally in a leaf chamber.

Plant Diseases

Mulberry plant is affected by fungi, viruses etc. If the plant is affected by 'white root rot' the plant becomes weak, the leaves wither off and some plants die. In such cases the diseased plant should be uprooted and burnt. In the 'leaf spot disease' the affected leaves have a number of circular or irregular brownish black spot and these leaves are unfit for feeding. Spraying suitable fungicides soon after picking the leaves and much before the next picking is advised in most of the these cases.

LIFE CYCLE OF A SILKWORM

Breeding and Hatching

The insect producing mulberry silk is a domesticated variety of silkworm belonging to the species Bombyx Mori. The life cycle of a silkworm is quite interesting. Male and female moth mate and female lays about 400 to 600 eggs which is called a laying. The life of a moth is between 3 and 10 days. The univoltine races produce only one generation during the spring and the second generation egg goes through a period of deep sleep or hybernation till the next spring. In the cases of bivoltine races the second generation eggs hatched produce larvae normally during summer but the third generation eggs undergo hybernation and hatch in only next spring thus producing only two generations in a year. In multivoltine races the life cycle is shortest because of the warmer ecological conditions where they are reared. They may yield as many as seven to eight generations in a year in tropical countries like India. Silkworm rearing is, therefore continuos in tropical areas whereas in sub-tropical or temperate zones it is mostly seasonal, lasting from spring to early autumn.

The eggs hatch within a period of 11 days. It is important to get disease free layings (DFLs). The diseased eggs would have high mortality rate. The disease will also spread to the rearings in nearby areas. The quality and quantity of the silk from the diseased worms would not be of acceptable standard. To ensure disease free layings, the mother moth is crushed and examined under a microscope. If the pebrine spores are present in the body of the mother moth it means the egg laid by her were affected by the same disease. Such layings are rejected and destroyed. This is done in certified breeding houses called Grainages. In silkworms a marked improvement in several characteristics of economic importance has been observed in first generation of hybrids—i.e., between breeds belonging to different regional races. Some of the advantages of hybrids are (i) larva period is shorter (ii) mortality is reduced (iii) leaf required per cocoon is low (iv) cocoon weight is high (v) filament length of fibre is longer.

Larva Stage

The larva which comes out of egg is a voracious eater. During the 22—24 days the larva increases its weight almost by 10,000 times. From a tiny speck it grows to become a 6 to 7 cm long worm. Nature has provided a built-in arrangement for the rapid increase in body-size of the silkworm. The process is known as moulting i.e., changing of the skin for four times. Each moulting requires 20 to 24 hrs. and during this period the worm does not eat. The period between hatching and first moulting is called first age or I instar and the period between first moulting and second moulting is called II age or II instar and so on. Thus there are five instars. First and second age are 3 days each, III age 3–4 days, IV age 4–5 days while V age 6–7 days. After the V age the worm stops eating and is mature to spin cocoon.

Process of silkworm rearing

The silk worms have to be reared with utmost care. Bacteria, some protozoans, virus and fungi attack the silkworms readily and any disease once breaks out spreads quickly. The rearing room and the equipment to be used for rearing should be thoroughly cleaned, washed with water and dried. Afterwards the equipment and the rearing room should be disinfected by spraying 2–4 per cent formalin solution. Before disinfecting, the crevices and holes in the room should be filled in and room should be made air-tight. After spraying, the room should be kept closed for 15–20 hours. Afterwards the room is kept open for almost 24 hours so that all traces of formalin vapour disappear. After two to three days from this disinfection the eggs can be brought for hatching.

Hatching of worms starts early in the morning. The hatched larvae should not be starved. They must be brushed on to a rearing tray having paraffin paper. This is done by sprinkling the chopped tender mulberry leaves of size 0.5 to 1 square cm over the hatched larvae. The larvae crawl on the leaves and after a few minutes the egg sheet is inverted over a rearing tray with paraffin paper so that the larvae get transferred on the rearing tray by using a feather. It is necessary to maintain at this stage a temperature of 27°–28° C and humidity upto 90%. If the room temperature is humidity less than required level, wet foam pads inside the rearing tray along sides should be kept and paraffin paper can be used to cover the tray. If room temperature is lower than required, heating with electric heaters or charcoal fire also becomes necessary. Apart from the controlled temperature and humidity the adequate bed spacing should be maintained for growing worms for their easy movement and avoiding congestion and resultant infighting. The regular cleaning of the bed to maintain the hygienic conditions is essential.

For feeding, cleaning, removal of left over leaves and excreta, shifting the worms for increasing bed spacing, etc: constant attention and labour is required. 95% of leaf consumption is during IV and V stage. The cultivators have therefore to ensure that the required quntity of leaves would be available from the farm. Adequate labour should also be available to harvest the leaves and feed them to the silk-worms. It is essential to maintain freshness and quality of the leaves during feeding. While tender leaves are fed in I and II age, the mature leaves are preferred in late age.

Mounting and Harvesting

The ripe worms are picked up and put to mountages where they complete the spinning of silk filament in a cocoon form in 2 or 3 days. The mountage in India are circular in nature and are made of bamboos. They are called chandrikas in regional language. A chandrika is generally of a size of 6' x 4' and can accommodate about 1000 larvae i.e., 40 to 50 silkowrms per square foot. The mountages are kept in shade. For good spinning the temperature around 22°C to 24°C and the humidity between 60 to 70 per cent is ideal. The worm anchors itself first to the mountage by oozing a very tiny droplet of silk fluid which immediately hardens and sticks to the mountage. Then by continuous movements of the head, silk fluid is excreted in minute quantities which goes on hardening to form a long continuous filament. The larva at first lays the foundation for the cocoon structure by weaving a preliminary web or the floss of the cocoon. The floss is univoltine and bivoltine is 2% of the weight of the cocoon while in multivoltine it is as high as 10%. Within 2 to 4 days process of spinning cocoon is complete. Once the spinning of cocoon is complete the larva inside the cocoon, undergoes metamorphosis in two days and becomes pupa. The pupa initially has very tender skin and within 2–3 days it hardens and becomes dark brown and the cocoon is thus ready for marketing. Thus it takes about ten days from the day of mounting to harvesting of cocoons. Marketing of these cocoons should be arranged immediately otherwise the pupa turns into moth inside the cocoon in a period of 4–5 days and comes out piercing the cocoon and thus destroying the silk filaments. These pierced cocoons are useless for getting the silk filament because the filament is continuous thread and it gets cut in small bits. It is then impossible to get a continuous filament for reeling. The pupa inside the cocoon has therefore to be killed or stifled by putting the cocoon in boiling water or is exposed to hot air dryer.

Rearing House

It is advisable to rear a greater number of layings at a time than to rear many batches of small number of layings. It is always beneficial to plan the rearing programme after taking into account the availability of leaves. There is need to have separate rearing space or rearing house.

The rearing house should have sufficient number of windows to permit cross ventilation. It is also necessary to make the rearing house airtight for proper disinfection. To rear a 400 to 500 dfls at a time a rearing house with a plinth area of 525 square meter or 32' to 16' with rearing hall of 30' x 15' is necessary. It should be a rat proof building with a ledge all around. The building should have verandah all round and glass windows and doors to provide good ventilation and light. The rearing house should be conveniently partitioned to maintain required temperature and humidity conditions.

Generally three types of rearings are known i) shelf rearing ii) shoot rearing and iii) floor rearing. In shelf rearing, rearing trays of convenient sizes are arranged on stands with eight to ten tiers. This method economises on space. In the case of shoot rearing, rearing is done in two or three tiers of conventient length and breadth of rearing beds. In case of floor rearing the rearing is done right on the floor or on a raised platform in beds of convenient length and breadth. Since the shelf rearing is commonly observed and preferred by the farmers the same is considered here while describing rearing process.

Silkworm Diseases and Pests

The silkworms are susceptible to various diseases and attack by pests and parasites. A few of them are described below:-

(i) Pebrine

This is also known as a pepper disease because the black or brown spots that appear on the diseased silkworms look like pepper grains. The disease is transmitted through the eggs by contact with the diseased silkworms and through the contaminated leaves.

(ii) Flacheria

This is said to be a bacterial disease. The symptoms are the larva loses appetite, becomes sluggish and grows slowly and its body shrinks.

(iii) Muscardine or Calcino

This is a fungal disease. The progress of the disease in the infected larva is very rapid. The larva loses appetite and becoms inactive, it ceases to move and generally dies within three to five days of infenction.

(iv) Uzi Fly (Tricholyga bambycin)

This is a dipteran fly of the family Tachinidae and is a serious pest of silkworm larvae and pupae. It is a parasite on silkworm and can caüse considerable damage to silkworm rearing. It is a large fly with prominent black and grey stripes and dark ebony in colour. Ordinarily the fly pest prefers late age (III to V age) silkworms for laying eggs. The most effective method of control is to prevent the entry of the fly into the rearing rooms by providing suitable nylon or mesh wire (fly proof) nets for doors, windows and ventilators wherever raring is done. The maggot infected larva and cocoon should be destroyed by burning.

Similarrly the ants, lizards, rats, squirrels and birds may attack the silkworms at different stages and appropriate precautions like providing ant wells, wire mesh for doors, windows etc., and keeping the mountages indoor respectively may help preventing their attack.

An attempt has been made in this chapter to highlight the certain statistical data i.e., production of mulberry cocoons acrage and silk production at World, National and State Level.

World Silk Scenario

Silk provides the much needed employment in several developing and labour rich countries. It is well known fact that over 25 countries in Asia, Africa and south Africa are at present envisaging or are actually engaged in sericultural projects of varying dimensions. As a sharp contrast to this trend, some European countries like France, Italy and Spain, which used to have a fairly large scale of sericulture are no longer engaged in mulberry planting and silkworm rearing[2]. The Tables 3.1 and 3.2 presented here may be seen for the trends in world production of green mulberry cocoons and raw silk proudction.

Ever since World War II, Japan's raw silk output has been on an incessant decline, despite the Japanese governments efforts to reverse the situation. Raw silk output hit its Peak (5,584 tonnes) in South Korea in 1977. However, the country's silk production started to decline in the 1980's. In 1986, South Korea produced merely, 1,650 tonnes of raw silk. One can easily see that raw silk production enjoys rapid growth mostly in the developing countries.

Table 3.1 : Table Showing the World Production of Green Mulberry Cocoons

	Different Years						
Country	*1980*	*1985*	*1986*	*1987*	*1988*	*1989*	*1990*
China	24800	3077500	328000	345000	394000	420000	478500
India	85208	76700	81600	86500	96471	110433	116672
Japan	73060	47300	41400	34700	29600	26890	24924
USSR	48906	52000	44000*	44000*	44000*	44000*	44000*
Republic of Korea	20035	10300	10300$	7200	5900	5400	5400
Brazil	8800	10700	10700$	11760	11800	11470	1582
Others	28291	30900	30900$	30900$	33519	22007	22007
Total	**845300**	**535400**	**546900**	**560060**	**615290**	**640200**	**707033**

Source:- Statistical Biennial, Silk in India, 1992 (Central Silk Brad, Bangalore).
* Estimated ;
$ 1985 data repeated.

Table 3.2 : Table Showing the World Mulberry Raw Silk Productions

(Tonnes)

Country	*Different Years*						
	1980	*1985*	*1986*	*1987*	*1988*	*1989*	*1990*
China	23485	32000	35700	35800	34400	40700	46400
India	4596$	7029	2905	8455	9683	10905	11487
Japan	16155	9592	8341	7864	6862	6078	5720
USSR	4254	4000	4000+	4000+	4000+	4000+	4094
Republic of Korea	3279	1850	1650	1608	1338	1200	1200@
Brazil	1284	1558	1780	1780+	1749	1697	1693
Others	2450	2671	2784	2874+	3288	2285	2285
Total	**55500**	**58700**	**62250**	**52381**	**61320**	**66865**	**72879**

Source:- Statistical Biennial, Silk in India, 1992 (Central Silk Brad, Bangalore).

$ Data refers to financial year from 1980 onwards.

\+ Estimated

* 1986 data repeated.

@ 1989 data repeated.

This is largely due to the low level of their economy, and the suitability of sericulture of family labour and low-paid rural labour. In addition, favourable weather conditions, less investment with quick profit and the high market demands all contributed greatly to the expansion of sericulture. The potential to enter the export market with cocoons, raw silk and finished goods also undoubtedly plays a role in the expansion of sericulture in these countries.

Though a big silk producing and consuming country, Japan can no longer produce enough raw silk to satisfy the need to its silk processing industry. In 1987, it imported 1,457 tonnes of raw silk and in 1989, 2,048 tonnes. With rapid industrialisation, South Korea has been trying to expand its production of printed fabrics, garments and other finished goods which are now exported to Hong Kong, Japan, the Middle East and United States.

It is noteworthy that in recent years some developing countries have also made positive efforts in developing value-added products, which has obviously increased their export volume. India is making much headway in becoming a supplier of silk garments (mainly women's dresses) and furnishing fabrics. Silk products from Thailand have also found their way to the Federal Republic of Germany, the United States, Holland and France.

It can be conclude that the Worldwide "silk craze" in the past few years has encouraged many developing countries to develop sericulture. According to the statistics provided by U.N.experts, by 1995 the world raw silk output will grow to 85,000 tonnes a 27 percent increase over the current world output.

Present Status of Sericulture in India

Sericulture today is a well established agro-based cottage industry. It is an effective tool for rural development as it generates income and employment. Out of the 5,76,000 villages in the country, sericulture is practised in about 50,000 (8.7%) villages providing employment to them belonging to the weaker sections of the society including scheduled castes and scheduled tribes.

India's Position in World Silk Production

The World silk production in the year 1987 was about 62,380 metrict tonnes of which Indian share was 8,455 (13.55%) tonnes according to International Silk Association. India ranked among the top three which includes China and Japan amounting for as much as 84 percent of the total global silk production. India ranks second (after China) among mulberry silk producers with a share of 14 per cent of the global production. She is the second largest producer of Tasar silk in the world[3]. Table 3.3 presents the mulberry acreage and raw silk production in India during 1980–81 to 1987–88.

Sericulture/silk industry plays a vital role in transferring wealth from richer sections of the society to poorer sections. Silk is consumed mostly by the affluent and the money so spent by them on purchase of silk is distributed among the sericulturists, reelers, twisters, weavers and traders. Summarry of the percentage distribution of money from sale of soft silk fabrics of weight 40, 50 and 60gms/mtr is given in Table 3.4 and in Graph 3.1.

Sericulture Progress through Plans

With advent of economic planning in the country, sericulture indus-

Table 3.3 : Table Showing the Facts about Indian Silk i.e., Mulberry Acreage and Raw Silk Production

Year	*Arcreage under Mulberry (hectares)*	*Production (Tonnes)*		
		Reeling	*Raw Silk*	*Silk Waste*
1980–81	1,70,000	58,208	4,593	1,376
1981–82	1,79,949	55,210	4,801	1,523
1982–83	1,96,848	66,811	5,214	1,825
1983–84	2,06,913	71,276	5,681	2,017
1984–85	2,14,838	74,875	6,895	2,464
1985–86	2,17,839	76,717	7,029	2,504
1986–87	2,29,758	81,573	7,905	2,837
1987–88	2,41,603	86,528	8,455	3,086

Source : Silkman's Companion, 1989, Central Silk Board, Bangalore.

Table 3.4 : Table Showing the Percentage Distribution of Money of Soft Silk Fabrics

(% share)

Category of Persons	*Soft Silk Fabric of*		
	40 gms/ mtr.	*50 gms/ mtr.*	*60 gms/ mtr*
Cocoon Producer	51.5	54.6	56.8
Reeler	6.2	6.6	6.8
Twister	8.2	8.7	9.1
Weaver	14.5	12.3	10.7
Trader	19.5	17.8	16.6
Total	**100.0**	**100.0**	**100.0**

Source : Silman's Companion, 1989, Central Silk Board, Bangalore.

try made progressive development through the consecutive plans. The following writeup trace out the scale of growth achieved by the Industry during the plan periods.

First–Five Year Plan (1951–52 to 1955–56)

Sericulture did not find a separate place in the 1st Plan which was included in the "Other Village Industries". During the First Five-Year Plan, grants-in-aid amounting to Rs.45.97 Lakh were sanctioned to the

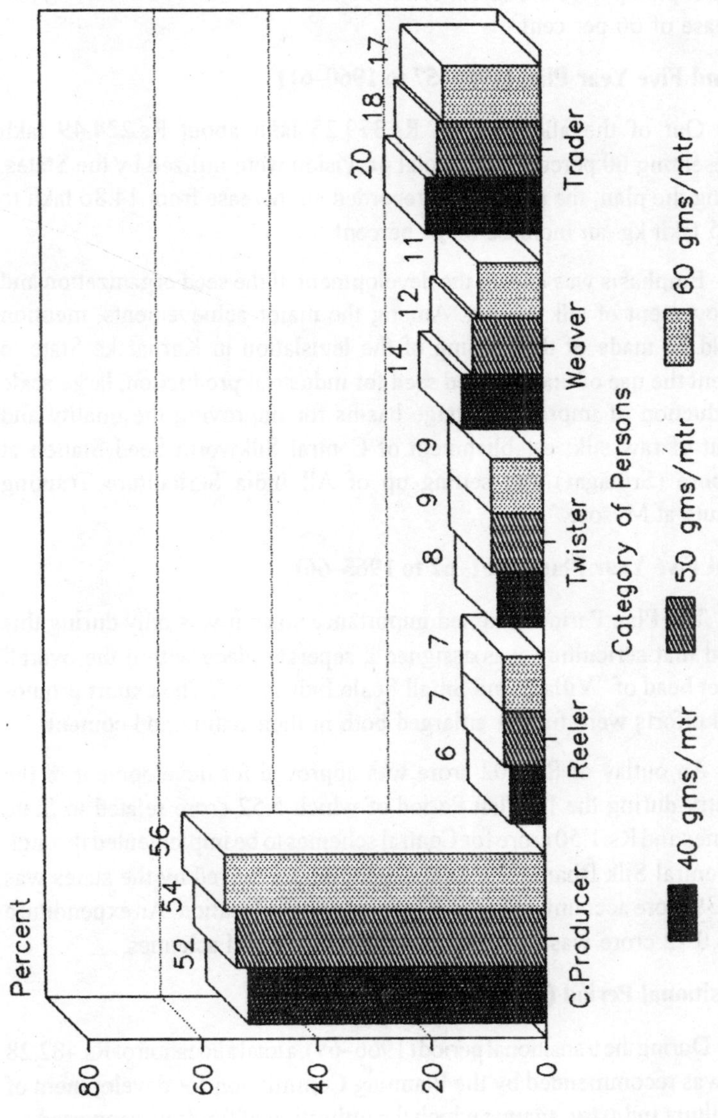

Graph 3.1 : Distribution of Money of Soft Silk Fabrics

State Governments, out of which only Rs.21.69 lakh were utilized. During the first plan period silk production rose from 8.94 to 14.86 lakh kg., an increase of 66 per cent.

Second Five Year Plan (1956–57 to 1960–61)

Out of the allocation of Rs.379.25 lakh about Rs.224.49 lakh representing 60 percent of the total provision were utilized by the States. During the plan, the production recorded an increase from 14.86 lakh to 16.95 lakh kg–an increase of 14 percent.

Emphasis was laid on the development of the seed organization and improvement of silk reeling. Among the major achievements, mention should be made of the passing of the legislation in Karnataka State to prevent the use of unexamined seed for industrial production, large scale introduction of improved cottage basins for improving the quality and output of raw silk; establishment of Central Silkworm Seed Station at pampore (Srinagar) and setting up of All India Sericulture Training Institute at Mysore.

Third Five Year Plan (1961–62 to 1965–66)

The Plan Period assumed importance since it was only during this period that sericulture was assigned a seperate place within the overall budget head of "Village and Small Scale Industries". The export promotional efforts were further enlarged both in their nature and content.

An outlay of Rs.7.02 crore was approved for development of the industry during the III Plan Period of which 5.52 crore related to State schemes and Rs.1.50 crore for Central schemes to be implemented through the Central Silk Board. The total expenditure incurred by the states was Rs.3.39 crore accounting for 61.4 percent of the allocation. An expenditure of Rs.0.72 crore was incurred in respect of Central schemes.

Transitional Period (1966 to 69)

During the transitional period (1966–69), a total allocation of Rs.482.28 lakh was recommended by the Planning Commission for development of sericulture industry, against which the utilisation of funds was reported by states as Rs.218.98 lakh. The production of raw silk at the end of 1968–69 stood at 23.20 lakh kgs.

Fourth Five Year Plan (1969–70 to 1973–74)

During the period, the allocation of states and central projects was Rs.8.39 lakh and Rs.130 lakh respectively. The broad objective of the IV Plan envisaged attainment of self sufficiency with regard to countries demand for raw silk through increased productivity, reduced cost of production through rationalization of production techniques and creating additional employment opportunity to about 4.00 lakh persons. The most important achievements during the Plan Periods are introduction of Oak tasar in the sub-Himalayan regions of the states of Jammu and Kashmir, Himachal Pradesh, Uttar Pradesh and Manipur and introduction of bivoltine rearing in the traditionally multi-voltine areas of Karnatakà, Tamil Nadu and West Bengal. By the end of the Plan Period Production of raw silk reached 28.94 lakh kg. and export earnings reached Rs.14.46 crore.

Fifth Five Year Plan (1974–75 to 1977–78)

The Planning Commission approved an outlay of Rs.25.54 crore during the V Plan Period. Out of this, a sum of Rs.1109.06 lakh was spent on State schemes and Rs.586.17 lakh on Central schemes.

A special scheme under the Central programmes was initiated in 1975–76 for introducing mulberry sericulture in backward areas by way of supplying mulberry cuttings/saplings at subsidised rates. The programme for introduction of bivoltine hybrids in the traditionally multivoltine states of Karnataka, Tamil Nadu, Andhra Pradesh and West Bengal was also initiated during the Plan Period consequent to the break through in silkworm rearing technology by the board's research institutions. In order to hasten the success of the above bivoltine programme and to supplement the State Government's efforts in respect of production and supply of high quality bilvoltine and multi- bivoltine hybrids/seeds, Central Silk Board during the Plan Period established 11 grainages. By the end of the Plan Period Production of raw silk reached the level of 37.11 lakh kg. and export earnings touched the level of Rs.33.06 crore.

Trasitional Period (1978–79)

The Planning Commission approved an allocation of Rs.728.05 lakh for development of sericulture industry in the State sector during 1978–79 against which the States sanctioned Rs.568.23 lakh and utilized Rs.510.36 lakh for the year. The overall production of raw silk increased to 41.77 lakh kg. from 37.11 lakh kg. during the previous year.

Annual Plan (1979–80)

An allocation of Rs.861.66 lakh was approved by the Planning Commission for development of Sericulture in the State sector against which an expenditure of Rs.762.28 lakh was recorded during the year. The production of raw silk increased by 6.28 lakh kg from 41.77 lakh kg. in 1978–79 to 48.05 lakh in 1979–80.

Sixth Five Year Plan (1980–81 to 84–85)

The Planning Commission approved an allocation of Rs.167.37 crore during the VI Plan Period. However, the year to year allocation approved under the central projects during the VI Plan Period amounted to Rs.40 crore. Thus, the allocation during the VI Plan Period amounted to Rs.207.37 crore. Out of this, a sum of Rs.89.23 crore was spent on State schemes and Rs.37.15 crore on Central Projects. By the end of the Plan Period, Production of raw silk reached the level of 76.73 lakh kg and silk export earnings to Rs.129.05 crore.

Seventh Five Year Plan (1985–86 to 1989–90)

The Planning Commission, Government of India approved an allocation of Rs.310.78 crore during the VII Plan Period. By the end of the Plan Period Production of raw silk reached the level of 120.16 tonnes and silk export earnings amounted to Rs.400.16 crore.

During the plan period, Intensive Sericulture Development Projects for mulberry were taken up for implementation in Orissa and West Bengal at a cost of Rs.427 lakh and Rs.967 lakh respectively for purposes of expansion of area under improved variety of mulberry, setting up of sound infrastructure for quality seed production, supply and marketing etc.

During 1989–90, the final year of the VII Plan Period, Central Silk Board with the financial assistance from World Bank and STC, for the development of mulberry sericulture in the country initiated the "National Sericulture Project" (NSP) at a total cost of Rs.555.3 crore. The Project envisages to bring an additional acreage of 57,600 hectares of land under mulberry cultivation in order to produce additional 6072 metric tonnes of mulberry raw silk by the end of Five Year Project Period.

Table 3.5 and 3.6 given below indicates the financial and Physical Progress achieved during each of the Plan/transitional periods.

Transitional Period (1990–91)

The Planning Commission, Government of India had approved on allocation of Rs.161.20 crores for development of sericulture both under State and Central Sector for the year 1990–91. During the year, production of raw silk increased to 12,665 tonnes over the preceeding year level of

Table 3.5 : Table Indicating the Financial Progress Achieved During Each of the Plan/Transitional Period

Financial Progress

(Rs. in lakhs)

Period	*Allocation*	*Provision sanctioned*	*Expenditure*
Central Project :			
2nd Plan	35.17	38.80	26.13
3rd Plan	150.00	76.58	72.32
Transitional period (1966–89)	70.24	71.04	62.32
4th Plan	130.00	99.56	81.61
5th Plan	861.20	788.00	586.17
Transitional Period (1978–80)	1320.00	---	110.46
6th Plan	3100.00	4000.00	3715.00
7th Plan	7000.00	---	8816.00**
State Schemes :			
2nd Plan	379.25	268.73	224.49
3rd Plan	552.01	471.43	339.42
Transitional period (1966–89)	482.28	307.63	218.98
4th Plan	839.00	763.40	593.38
5th Plan	1693.18	---	1109.06
Transitional period (1978–80)	1589.71	---	1259.26
6th Plan	13637.00	---	8922.67
7th Plan	24078.00	25299.69	20588.63

Source : Statistical Biennial, Central Silk Board, Bangalore, 1992.

** Includes an expenditure of Rs. 240.00 lakh under National Sericulture Project (NSP) initiated during 1989–90.

Table 3.6 : Table Showing the Production of Raw Silk

Physical Progress

Year	*Kinds of Silk*				
	Mulberry	*Tesar*	*Eri*	*Muga*	*Total*
1951–52	6.25	1.24	1.00	0.45	8.94
1960–61	11.85	1.79	1.00	0.39	15.13
1965–66	15.45	2.62	2.01	0.57	20.65
1968–69	17.81	2.56	2.14	0.69	23.20
1973–74	24.21	2.57	1.41	0.75	28.94
1977–78	31.86	4.34	0.56	0.35	27.11
1979–80	41.93	3.84	1.83	0.45	48.05
1984–85	68.95	4.44	2.79	0.55	76.73
1985–86	70.29	4.64	3.52	0.52	78.97
1986–87	79.05	5.48	3.92	0.55	89.00
1987–88	84.55	4.63	5.22	0.58	94.98
1988–89	96.83	3.58	5.65	0.45	106.51
1989–90	109.05	4.65	5.89	0.57	120.16
1990–91	114.87	4.84	6.24	0.70	125.50

Source : Statistical Biennieal, Central Silk Board, Bangalore, 1992.

12,016 tonnes. On the export front, the achievement was Rs.440.3 crores over the previous year's achievement of Rs.400.61 crores.

Transitional Period (1991–92)

For the year 1991–92 the allocation approved both under State and Central Sector has been Rs.211.88 crores and physical targets suggested are production of 14,060 metric tonnes of raw silk and export earnings to Rs.600.00 crores.

Eighth Five Year Plan (1992–93 to 1996–97)

The Planning Commission, Government of India had constituted a sub-group on sericulture for formulation of sericulture development programmes for VIII Plan. The final outlay proposed for development of sericulture during VIII Plan both under Central and State sector is Rs.860.76 crores. Since the eighth five year plan is in implementation details about production and other information is not known.

Sericulture in Andhra Pradesh

Sericulture is an ancient activity in India dating back to the second century BC. The weaving of silk has become an integral part of Indian culture and tradition. In 1987, India overtook Japan to becomes the world's second largest mulberry silk producer with 13% of world production.

In 1975, the start of the V Plan, Andhra Pradesh was a mere speck on the sericulture map of India. Producing only around 300 tonnes of mulberry silk cocoons. Today Andhra Pradesh is the second largest producer of cocoons in the country, with an annual production of 30,000 tonnes and providing employment approximately 10 lakh persons.

The industry has taken roots in almost every district more particularly in Krishna, Cuddapah, Nellore, Kurnool, West Godavari, Karimnagar, Mahaboobnagar, Medak, Adilabad, Srikakulam, Anantapur and Chittoor. The industry has been playing a vital role in improving the economy of small and marginal farmers in these districts. The area under mulberry plantation which was stagnating around 3,000 acres until 1973–74 has increased to 20,430 acres by the end of 1978–79 and further to 1,06,924 acres at the end of 1987–88. The sudden expansion in the area under mulberry plantation has been possible mainly due to the State Government's initiative in implementing special development programmes for sericulture under the Drought Prone Area Programme (DPAP). Mulberry cultivation is 80%–90% under irrigated condition in the State[4].

An Indo-Swiss mulberry sericulture development project is being implemented in Andhra Pradesh at a total cost of Rs.141.11 lakh which includes Swiss grant to the extent of Rs.131.03 lakh.

The State has proposed implementation of National Sericulture Development Project with external assistance at a total cost of Rs.136.40 crore over a period of five years. The project envisages to cover 10,000 hect. of area under the mulberry for production of additional 10,940 tonnes of cocoons and 960 metric tonnes of raw silk. The various infrastructure facilities proposed under the project are 50 seed farms, seven P2/P1 grainages, 150 Chawkie rearing centres, seven cocoon markets, 430 technical service centres, one training school, one research unit, three reeler training centres,one reeling unit, one silk exchange and seven cocoon testing units[5].

There is fast growth in the area under mulberry, raw silk production, number of sericulture villages and as well as number of sericulturists. In order to have a comparative picture the Table 3.7 may be examined.

Table 3.7 : Table Showing the Increase in Mulberry Acreage Raw Silk Production and Sericulturists in A.P.

Sl.No.	*Mulberry Sector*	*1975-76*	*1991-92*
1.	Acrage under Mulberry	4,890	1,06,723
2.	Raw silk production M.T. (Based cocoon production)	234	2454.720
3.	Actual Silk Production in the State (M.T.)	---	433.390
4.	No. of Sericulture Villages	468	10,189
5.	No. of Sericulturists	7896	1,33,946
	i) Marginal	5711	1,14,108
	ii) Small Farmers	2122	12,776
	iii) Big Farmers	63	7062

Source : Credit tie-up—The A.P. experience by Rachel Chatterjee.

Sericulture industry has got the maximum potential of providing employment opportunities to the people. The Table 3.8 and Graph 3.2 presented here highlight the number of families depend on sericulture as well as community-wise break-up.

Table 3.8 : Showing the No. of Families and Community-wise Break-up of Sericulturists

Sl.No.	*Year*	*SC*	*ST*	*Others*	*Total*
1.	1986–87	8205	3952	56048	68205
	% to total	(12.0)	5.8	82.2	100.0
2.	1987–88	10092	4399	58137	72628
	% to total	(13.9)	(6.1)	(80.0)	(100.0)
3.	1988–89	12537	7535	77423	97495
	% to total	(12.9)	(7.7)	(79.4)	(100.0)
4.	1989–90	14460	9512	99486	123458
	% to total	(11.7)	(7.7)	(80.6)	(100.0)

Source : Credit tie-up—The A.P. experience by Rachel Chatterjee.

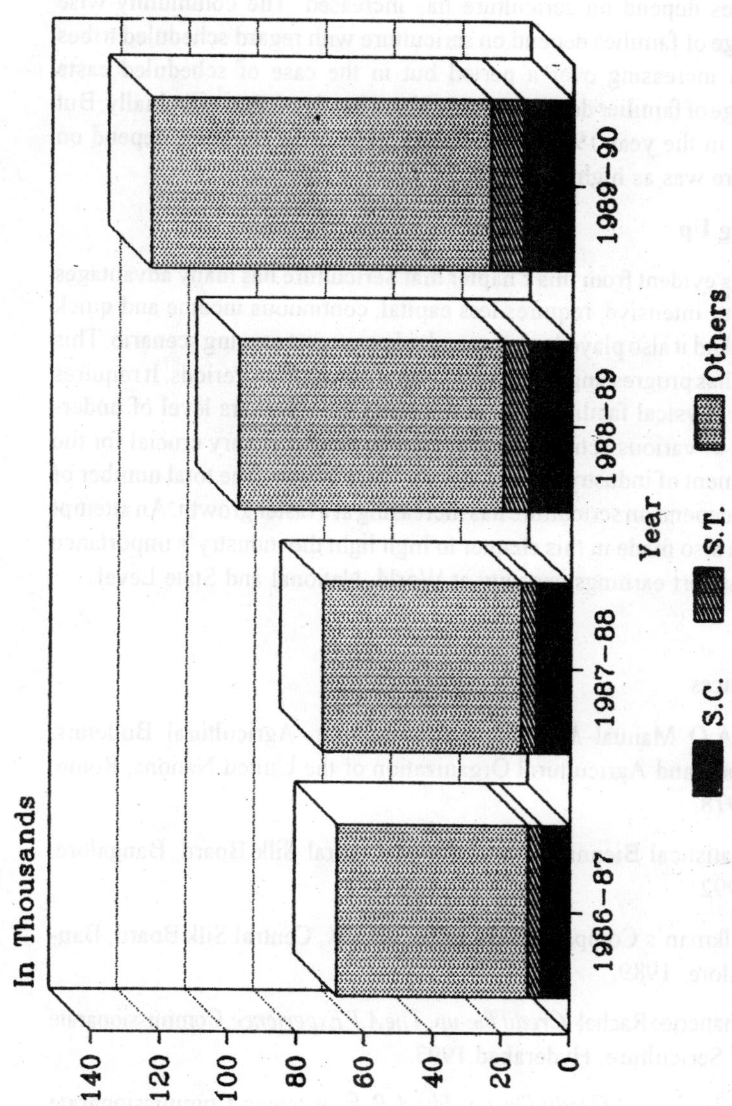

Graph 3.2 : Sericulturist in AP : Distribution Among Communities

The Table 3.8 reveal that for a period of five years the total number of families depend on sericulture has increased. The community-wise percentage of families depend on sericulture with regard scheduled tribes has been increasing over a period but in the case of scheduled caste percentage of families depend on sericulture has decreased marginally. But however in the year 1987–88 the percentage of SC families depend on sericulture was as high as 13.9%.

Summing Up

It is evident from this Chapter that Sericulture has many advantages like labour intensive, requires less capital, continuous income and quick returns. And it also played very crucial role in export earning scenario. This industry has progressing year after year and during Plan Periods. It requires not only physical facilities and at the same time farmers level of understanding of various activities. Education as a input is very crucial for the development of industry as well as individual farmer. The total number of families depend on sericulture has increasing at a faster growth. An attempt has been also made in this chapter to high light the industry's importance and its export earnings capacity at World, National and State Level.

Rerferences

1. F.A.O Manual–*Manuals on Sericulture,* Agricultural Bulletins, Food and Agricultural Organization of the United Nations, Rome, 1978.
2. Statistical Biennial–*Silk in India*, Central Silk Board, Bangalore, 1992.
3. Silkman's Companion–*Statistics on Silk*, Central Silk Board, Bangalore, 1989.
4. Chatterjee Rachel–*Credit Tie-up: The A.P Experience*, Commissionarate of Sericulture, Hyderabad, 1993.
5. ————, *Credit Tie-up: The A.P. Expereince*, Commissionarate of Sericulture, Hyderabad, 1993.

4

EDUCATION AND ECONOMIC DEVELOPMENT

"An Illiterate Person has hundreds of enemies: Epidemics, hunger, disorder, humiliation. Illiteracy is a curse to humanity".

— H.M. Phillips

Education is in fact a multiple process, developing and promoting social, economic, health, cultural and other consciousness among human beings also education is a vital medium to imbibe, foster and perpetuate values in man. Education is in fact a never ending process and in the real sense meant to humanise humanity. Lynn Smith[1] defind education "as a process whereby the socially approved part of cultural heritage is transmitted from one generation to the following one and whereby newly acquired knowledge is diffused among members of society".

The Concept of Human Capital

Capital, broadly defined is anything that yields a flow of services over time. It is a produced means of production, used for further production in the economy[2]. In this sense, knowledge can be treated as capital. Knowledge may be embodied in physical forms or in human beings for effective utilization in the economy. Knowledge embodied in physical form takes the character of physical capital in particular and of technological progress in general while knowledge embodied in human beings forms

human capital. Both forms of capital yield a flow of services and their possession and application provide income to their owners through their services. Knowledge is used here in a broad sense. It is not only the fund of information and the flow of information but also skill, the ability to use ones knowledge effectively in performance.

There is overwhelming evidence that human capital is one of the key to rapid development. Moreover, improvements in health, education and nutrition reinforce each other. The principal asset of the people is labour. Education increases the productivity of this asset. The consequent results precipitated, as many studies showed, is higher income. Recent research studies also points to a strong link between education and economic development.

Many people do not work for wages and many of them are self-employed in agriculture or in small family enterprises. Educated farmers are more likely to adopt new technologies and virtually all studies on agricultural productivity showed that better educated farmers get a higher return on their land.

Education has a unique role in the process of human development. Education is a critical means to gain knowledge and skills. Economists have repeatedly stressed the importance of giving due consideration to the human factor in socio-economic development. Human capital revolution of the 1960s in economic literature has further exalted the importance of education as a component of human resource development.

Education effects development through its enduring impact on various dimensions of cognitive competence. These cognitive skills affect an individuals productive behaviour and ability to use the products of technological change eg: high yield variety seeds, fertilizers and pesticides correctly[3]. Education and comprehension are valuable for farmers involved in mulberry cultivation and cocoon rearing. Farmers who can read, write and comprehend can allocate inputs efficiently and thus increase productivity[4]. Education help farmers to establish the profitability of past activities and the risk of future ones. Reading and writing help farmers keep records and properly apply modern agricultural technologies such as agricultural chemicals, inorgnaic fertilizers and new seed varieties. Cotlear[5] stressed the relationship between education and technological innovation by emphasizing the importance of non-cognitive aspects of education, such as receptivity to new ideas, that put the educated farmers more easily in contact with new technologies.

The practice of sericulture comprises of two major activities namely mulberry cultivation for raising of leaf crop to feed the silkworms and rearing of silkworms to produce the cocoons which is the raw material for the silk reeling industry. Mulberry cultivation is agriculture in nature, the operations involved being simple, straight and easy to be carried out. On the other hand, silkworm rearing is a quite complicated process, calling for a great management skills with due understanding of the various technological aspects involved. The silkworm which has been domesticated and evolved over many thousands of generations, to produce substantial quantities of silk in a very short period, is indeed very delicate and requires careful handling during the process of rearing.

This chapter mainly deals with the issues of respondents ability in managing the different activities involved in mulberry cultivation and cocoon rearing. *The analysis and presentation of data pertaining to sericulture is correlated with the different levels of formal education acquired by the respondents.* The levels of education has been classified into five categories namely (*i*) illiterate (*ii*) Primary (*iii*) Middle (*iv*) High School and (*v*) Higher Secondary.

The impact of formal education on sericulture farmers is broadly divided into two parts. All the issues pertaining to mulberry cultivation are discussed in first part and the issues relating to cocoon rearing have been discussed in the second part.

I

Management of Mulberry Cultivation

Mulberry is a drought resistant plant capable of thriving under a variety of agro-climatic conditions. And at the same time, it is also sensitive, responding extremely well to optimum agricultural inputs but showing practically no growth when plant nutrients and moisture begin to operate as limiting factors. This is evident from the fact that under poor rain fall conditions (625–750 mm) prevailing in South India, the leaf yield is of the order of only 3,000–3,500 Kgs per hectare, whereas under assured irrigation and appropriate fertilizer application, it can be stepped upto 30,000 kgs or nearly ten times more. Further, mulberry under South Indian conditions, unlike in temperature regions like Japan, Korea and USSR gives continuous growth almost throughout the year, because of optimum temperature conditions and good sunshine available[6].

Before entering into any new occupation other than their traditional one, people must have formed an opinion as to what is the reason for adopting particular one. An enquiry is set in the survey to ascertain the reason for taking up sericulture as an occupation with the sample respondents. It is observed that cultivators shift their croping pattern when they get more income out of less capital investment provided other physical conditions suits. The Table 4.1 presents the response pattern opined by the respondents.

Table 4.1 : Distribution of Respondents Based on the Reasons

Sl. No.	*Reasons*	*Selected Villages*		
		Maluguru	*Tumakunta*	*Total*
1.	More income with less capital investment	142 (83.53)	17 (94.4)	159 (84.57)
2.	More number of people can be employed	11 (6.47)	---	11 (5.85)
3.	Everybody is taking up so I too	15 (8.82)	1 (5.6)	16 (8.51)
4.	Sericulture department officials motivated	2 (1.18)	---	2 (1.06)
	Total	**170 (100.0)**	**18 (100.0)**	**188 (100.0)**

(Figures in paranthesis indicate percentages)

It is revealed from the Table that 84.57% of respondents opined that by cultivation of sericulture they can earn more money with a limited financial investment which is an obvious reason. At the same time 5.85% of respondents revealed that more people can be employed from their household members while the farmer is engaged in mulberry cultivation, his family–which may consist of his wife, adult children, parents find work for each of the family member. The sericulture families of selected villages have ample reasons to be happy that they have taken up this occupation which provides them economic security besides deep emotional satisfaction.

Before embarking on sericulture the farmers were used to raise sugarcane and coarse food grains. Mulberry cultivation and cocoon rearing is completely new task for these farmers. How this activity absorbed and to what extent sericulture department played the role of an extension agent is a debatable point. For this, a question is introduced in the survey to elicit the motive behind the farmer to raise mulberry garden. The data is exhibited in Table 4.2.

Table 4.2 : Distribution of Respondents on Whose Advise Mulberry Planted

Sl. No.	*Reasons*	*Selected Villages* *Maluguru*	*Tumakunta*	*Total*
1.	Extension Officer advise	42 (24.70)	---	42 (22.34)
2.	Observing neighbours/ relatives	128 (75.30)	18 (100.0)	146 (77.66)
	Total	**170 (100.0)**	**18 (100.0)**	**188 (100.0)**

(Figures in paranthesis indicate percentages)

It is observed from the Table that 22.34% of the sampled respondents stated that on the advise of extension officer they started mulberry cultivation. When ever there is innovation in the agriculture, farmer tend to adopt by consulting neighbouring farmers and relatives who are already getting economic returns. This demonstrative effect is much faster than persuing kind of extension method. A significant portion 77.66% of respondents reveal that they are inclined to take up mulberry cultivation after consulting their co-farmers and relatives belonging to farthest places like some parts of Ramnagar, Sidlaghata of Karnataka State. To beginwith, few farmers started raising mulberry on an experimental basis. Those farmers are belong to upper caste and progressive farmers.

Mulberry farming which is entirely new occupation to the farmers who are started cultivating mulberry, need certain abilities and shrudness in understanding and implementation of different works, knowledge about different activities which are very essential. Those who can absorb and imbibe the knowledge by reading print material like pamphlets, bulletins can able to prosper. Whether this basic knowledge is prevelent among the mulberry cultivators or not and if so with what category of cultivators this knowledge is vested and what are their characteristics ?

To start with, simple questions were asked to the respondents about their awareness of the type of soil in which you are raising mulberry? what type of plantation system you are following? for plantation whether used cuttings or nursery raised plants? etc. For this type of simple questions, many respondents answered correctly and there was no much variation. After preparation of the field, cuttings have to be planted. It is important to see that the cuttings are placed deep and the soil around well compacted, leaving just one inch of the cutting exposed to environment. Whether the respondents are well aware of these tips or not is enquired through survey. The answers are recoded and numeric "1" is given for correct answer and numeric "2" is given for incorrect answer. The response pattern can be seen from Table 4.3.

Table 4.3 : Distribution of Respondents on the Knowledge of Depth of Cuttings

Sl. No.	*Reasons Pattern*	*No. of persons responded*
1.	Correct	163 (86.70)
2.	Incorrect	25 (13.30)
	Total	**188 (100.0)**

(Figures in paranthesis indicate percentages)

It is evident from the Table that 86.70% of respondents gave correct answer and 13.30% stated incorrect answer. Respondent's educational variable is correlated with the knowledge about the depth of cuttings. The results are presented in Table 4.4.

Farmers belonging to middle, SSC and higher secondary educational level gave cent percent correct answer. Among primary educated farmers 98.46% gave correct answer leaving one farmer who has revealed incorrect answer. Even among the illiterate farmers 52.94% were stated correct answer. This indicates that the knowledge about the depth of cutting is general and essential to each and every farmer.

It is also very essential to have knowledge about the high yielding variety of mulberry. In order to know the awareness of this aspect, the respondents were probed in this matter. Table 4.5 reveal that 53.72% of respondents were aware and 46.28% of respondents were not aware of any high–yielding variety of mulberry plants. As regards the name of the high yielding variety of mulberry, about 41.49% of respondents stated that they were aware of M–5 variety and 12.23% of respondents stated that they

Table 4.4 : Respondent's Educational Level and Knowledge About the Depth of Cuttings

Sl. No.	*Educational Level*	*Response Pattern*		
		Correct	*Incorrect*	*Total*
1.	Illiterate	27 (52.94)	24 (47.06)	51 (100.0)
2.	Primary	64 (98.46)	1 (1.54)	65 (100.0)
3.	Middle	34 (100.0)	---	34 (100.0)
4.	S.S.C.	27 (100.0)	---	27 (100.0)
5.	Higher Secondary	11 (100.0)	---	11 (100.0)
	Total	**163 (86.70)**	**25 (13.30)**	**188 (100.0)**

(Figures in paranthesis indicate percentages)

were aware about M–5 as well K2 varieties. Impact of educational variable on respondents is again analysed and correlated with this item. The analysis is presented in Table 4.5 and in Graph 4.1.

Table 4.5 : Impact of Education on the Awareness about High-Yielding Variety

(No. of Respondents)

Sl. No.	*Educational Level*	*Awareness about Varieties Plant Varieties*			
		M–5	*M–5 & K2*	*Not aware of any HYU*	*Total*
1.	Illiterate	2 (3.92)	1 (1.96)	48 (94.11)	51 (27.12)
2.	Primary	29 (44.61)	2 (3.07)	34 (52.30)	65 (34.57)
3.	Middle	26 (76.47)	4 (11.76)	4 (11.76)	34 (18.08)
4.	S.S.C.	16 (59.25)	10 (37.03)	1 (3.70)	27 (14.36)
5.	Higher Secondary	5 (45.45)	6 (54.55)	---	11 (5.85)
	Total	**78 (41.49)**	**23 (12.23)**	**87 (46.27)**	**188 (100.0)**

(Figures in paranthesis indicate percentages)

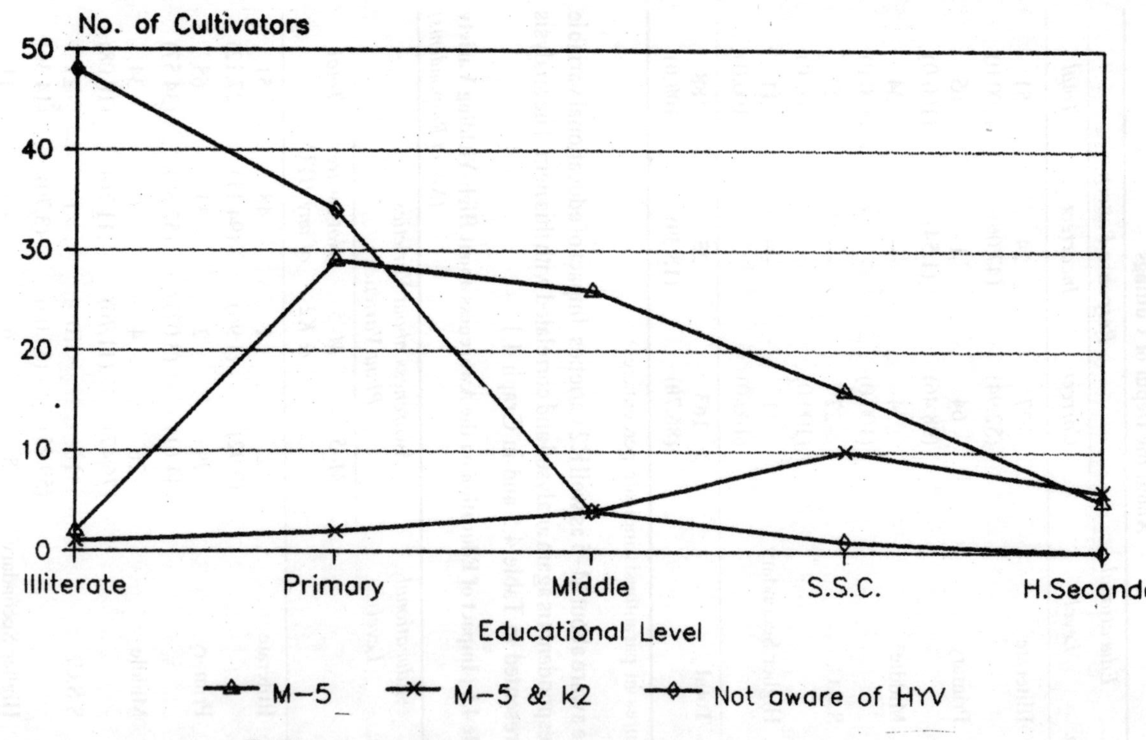

Graph : 4.1 : Awareness about the High-Yielding Variety

It is deduced from the analysis that 94.11% of illiterate farmers were not aware of the high yielding variety of mulberry plant. Out of 51 illiterate farmers exist among the sample, 5.88% farmers only named the high yielding variety. Whereas the percentage of awareness of high–yielding variety was 47.68% among primary, 88.23% among middle, 96.28% among SSC and 100.0% among higher secondary educated farmers. Knowledge about the variety of mulberry planted was highly correlated with the educational level of the sericulturists since r value = .3127.

Mulberry falls under the category of perennial crops and once it is properly planted and raised, it can come to full yielding capacity during the second year and last for over 15 years in the field without any significant deterioration in the yield of leaf. Some times there is a possibility of pest attack. If a farmer is fully aware of different kinds of pests, immediately without spoiling the crop further, he can be control it. Knowledge about different kinds of pests that affect mulberry was enquired. The data is presented in Table 4.6.

Table 4.6 : Distribution of Respondents' Knowledge about Crop Diseases

Sl. No.	*Name of the Disease*	*No. of farmers responded*
1.	Leaf Rust	5 (2.66)
2.	Leaf Spot	21 (11.17)
3.	Root knot	13 (6.91)
4.	Above all	149 (79.25)
	Total	**188 (100.0)**

(Figures in paranthesis indicate percentages)

The knowledge among cultivators about the pests is very high as 79.25% of respondents revealed that they were aware about important diseases that attack frequently. Whereas 2.66%, 11.17%, and 6.91% of respondents stated that they were aware only about leaf rust, leaf spot and root knot respectively. The similar set of data have been subjected to analysis with regard to the educational level of cultivators through correlation. The analysis is presented in Table 4.7.

It is revealed from analysis that 66.66%, 83.07%, 67.64%, 100.0% and 100.0% belonging to the category of illiterate, primary, middle, SSC and higher secondary educated respondents respectively were aware of all

Table 4.7 : Level of Education and Awareness about Different Diseases

Sl. No.	Educational Level	Awareness of Different Diseases				
		Leaf Rust	Leaf Spot	Root Knot	All	Total
1.	Illiterate	3 (5.88)	9 (17.64)	5 (9.80)	34 (66.66)	51 (27.12)
2.	Primary	2 (3.07)	7 (10.76)	2 (3.07)	54 (83.07)	65 (34.57)
3.	Middle	---	5 (14.70)	6 (17.64)	23 (67.64)	34 (18.08)
4.	S.S.C.	---	---	---	27 (100.0)	27 (14.36)
5.	Higher Secondary	---	---	---	11 (100.0)	11 (5.85)
	Total	**5 (2.66)**	**21 (11.17)**	**13 (6.91)**	**149 (79.25)**	**188 (100.0)**

(Figures in paranthesis indicate percentages)

important diseases which affect mulberry plantation. In this variable a strong association was found between level of education and the knowledge of diseases. The analysis reveal that when the level of education increases the knowledge of pests and diseases also increases correspondingly. And between the variables the positive association was found strong since its r value = .3127.

Timely application and adequate doses of manure/fertilizer is an important item through which it would be possible to reap optimum quantity of leaf. Organic manure should be applied at the rate of 4 tonnes per acre and it should be thoroughly incorporated in the soil. In addition to bulk organic manure, chemical fertilizers should also be applied like Nitrogen, Phosphorus, and Potassium (NPK). The farmers were enquired about the application of organic manure and inorganic fertilizers to the mulberry gardens. The data collected is presented in Table 4.8 and 4.9.

It can be seen from the Table 4.8 that 9.57% of cultivators did not use organic manure in adequate doses, whereas 54.78% of cultivators use sufficient doses. There were 35.63% of respondents who use above normal quantity with regard to organic fertilizers. It can also be seen from Table 4.9 that 78.72% of respondents use upto adequate doses whereas 21.27% of respondents use more than adequate doses of inorganic fertilizers. It is

Table 4.8 : Distribution of Respondents on the Use of Organic Manure

Sl. No.	*No. of Carts Used per acre*	*No. of Farmers*
1.	Less than 5 carts	18 (9.57)
2.	6 – 10 carts	103 (54.78)
3.	11–20 carts	60 (31.91)
4.	21–25 carts	7 (3.72)
	Total	**188 (100.0)**

(Figures in paranthesis indicate percentages)

(Note : One cart of manure is approximately 400–500 kgs.)

Table 4.9 : Distribution of Respondents on the Use of Inorganic Fertilizers

Sl. No.	*No. of kgs. used per acre*	*No. of Farmers*
1.	Upto 100 kgs.	148 (78.72)
2.	101–150 kgs.	34 (18.08)
3.	151–200 kgs.	6 (3.19)
	Total	**188 (100.0)**

(Figures in paranthesis indicate percentages)

generally felt that even if farmers use organic manure and they use inorganic fertilizers slightly more than adequate doses, but they would not use less than the prescribed quantum as it affect the growth and yield of the mulberry garden.

With regard to use of manure and fertilizer for mulberry garden, the impact of education is found marginally significant. Because it is critical and important input on which future activities depend, no farmer can ignore this component.

It can be concluded in this part that maximization of mulberry leaf yield per unit area will lead to the realization of two most important objectives namely (i) increase cocoon production per acre and (ii) reduction in cost of production. There is a high correlation between the education variable with certain other variables in regard to mulberry crop which needs different aspects of knowledge. And there are few items where there is marginal significance of educational impact. To some extent cultivation of mulberry garden is more or less like any agricultural activity and the importance of educational input has not been felt much. Therefore, it should be the primary aim of every sericulturist to ensure maximum leaf yield from mulberry crop. It is also realised after analysis of data that all measures taken to maximise leafyield, simultaneously help to improve the quality of leaves which automatically secures an insurence against cocoon crop losses at the later stage of silkworm rearing.

II

Management of Silkworm Rearing

Silkworm rearing is quite complicated process, encompassing different management skills with due understanding of the various technical aspects involved. Therefore, the job of rearing highly productive silkworms is a tough task for the farmers.

Until 1970, the average yield of cocoons for 100 disease free layings (comprising roughly about 40,000 eggs) was of the order of only 20-25 kgs as against 60-65kgs in temperate regions like Japan, Korea, USSR etc. An analysis of the poor coocon crop results in India indicated low values for the two important components that go to make the yield, namely (i) the number of cocoons harvested per laying and (ii) the average weight of the cocoons[7]. In the past, only about 50 per cent of the hatched larvae in the laying spun the cocoons successfully and the average cocoon weight was hardly 1 to 1.25 gms. If the layings are richer and the average number of eggs present goes upto 500, the yield will also correspondingly increase from 51 kgs to 63.25 kgs per 100 disease free layings. It can go still higher, if the number of cocoons harvested from a laying could be stepped up further. Thus, the key to bumper cocoon harvests lies in the skills of management of silkworm rearing aimed at achieving higher values for the above two components, namely, increased number of cocoons from a laying and higher cocoon weight.

From time to time Directorate of Sericulture as well as Central Sericultural Research and Training Institute, Mysore are propogating new varieties and update rearing technologies. To impart this new knowledge specific training modules are prepared for the benefit of farmers. At the same time printed booklets and pamphlets are distributed at the seed grainages, and at cocoon markets. The farmers who are educated upto primary could able to decode the information and intern implement in their ventures. The following discussion will examine how far educated farmers are better than illiterate farmers in imbibing and implementing new technologies.

The sampled farmers were enquired that how many times in a year they rear silkworms and number of disease free layings per crop. The data collected from the cultivators is presented in Table 4.10 and in Graph 4.2.

Table 4.10 : Distribution of Respondents and Number of Times doing Rearing in a Year

Sl. No.	*Educational Level*	*Frequency of Rearing*				*Total*
		1–2 Times	*3–4*	*5–8*	*9–12*	
1.	Illiterate	13 (25.49)	38 (74.51)	---	---	51 (27.13)
2.	Primary	10 (15.38)	53 (81.54)	2 (3.07)	---	65 (34.57)
3.	Middle	3 (8.82)	28 (82.35)	3 (8.82)	---	34 (18.05)
4.	S.S.C.	3 (11.11)	17 (62.96)	4 (14.81)	3 (11.11)	27 (14.36)
5.	Higher Secondary	1 (9.09)	7 (63.63)	2 (18.18)	1 (9.09)	11 (5.85)
	Total	**30 (15.96)**	**143 (76.06)**	**11 (5.85)**	**4 (2.13)**	**188 (100.0)**

(Figures in paranthesis indicate percentages)

It is revealed from Table 4.10 that 15.96%, 76.06%, 5.85% and 2.13% respondents were rearing worms between 1-2, 3-4, 5-8 and 9-12 times respectively in a year. It can also be observed that large number of farmers (76.06%) reared 3-4 times in a year. Highest percentage of farmers (25.49%) who were illiterate, reared between 1-2 crops which is least number of times when compared to the educated farmers. It is possible for educated farmers to rear above 5 crops in a year.

Data is also collected from farmers to enquire that how many disease free layings per crop a farmer rears. The data are exhibited in Table 4.11 and in Graph 4.3.

The data revealed that majority (47.34%) of respondents were rearing between 101-200 dfls per crop. There were also 37.76% of respondents who rear less than 100 dfls. Within the category of illiterate farmers, 62.74% of cultivators were rearing less than 100 dfls. Thus, a positive correlation exists between education and number of dfls reared

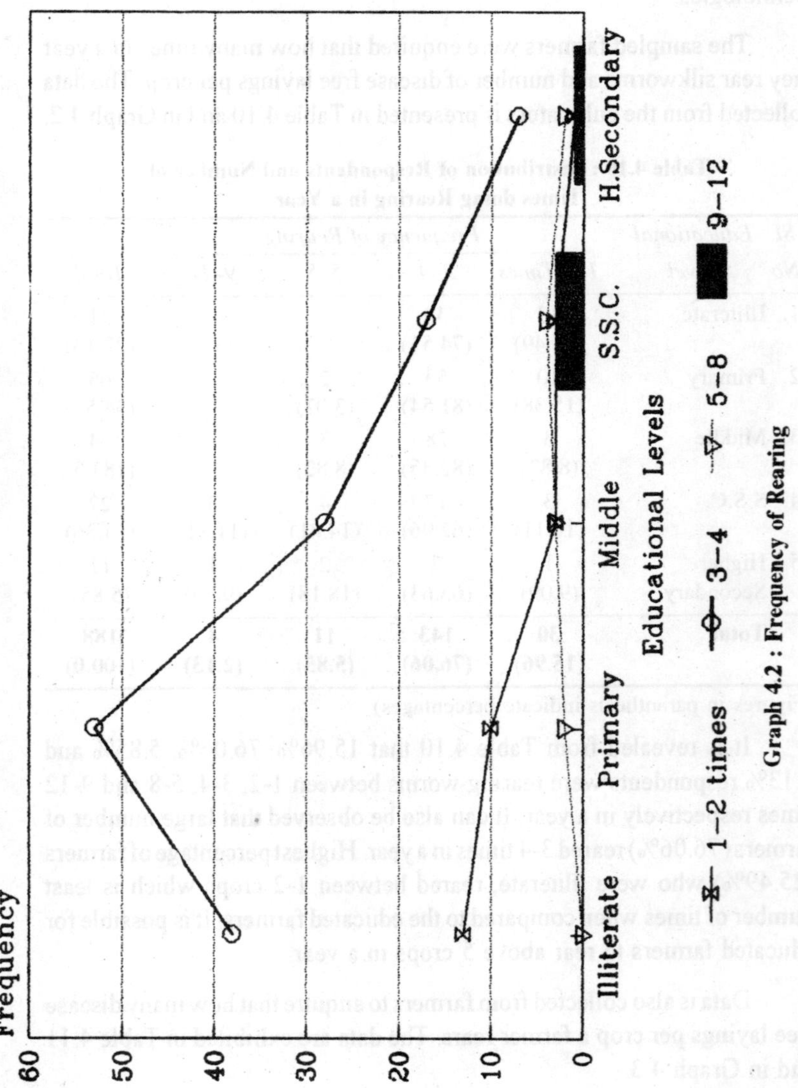

Graph 4.2 : Frequency of Rearing

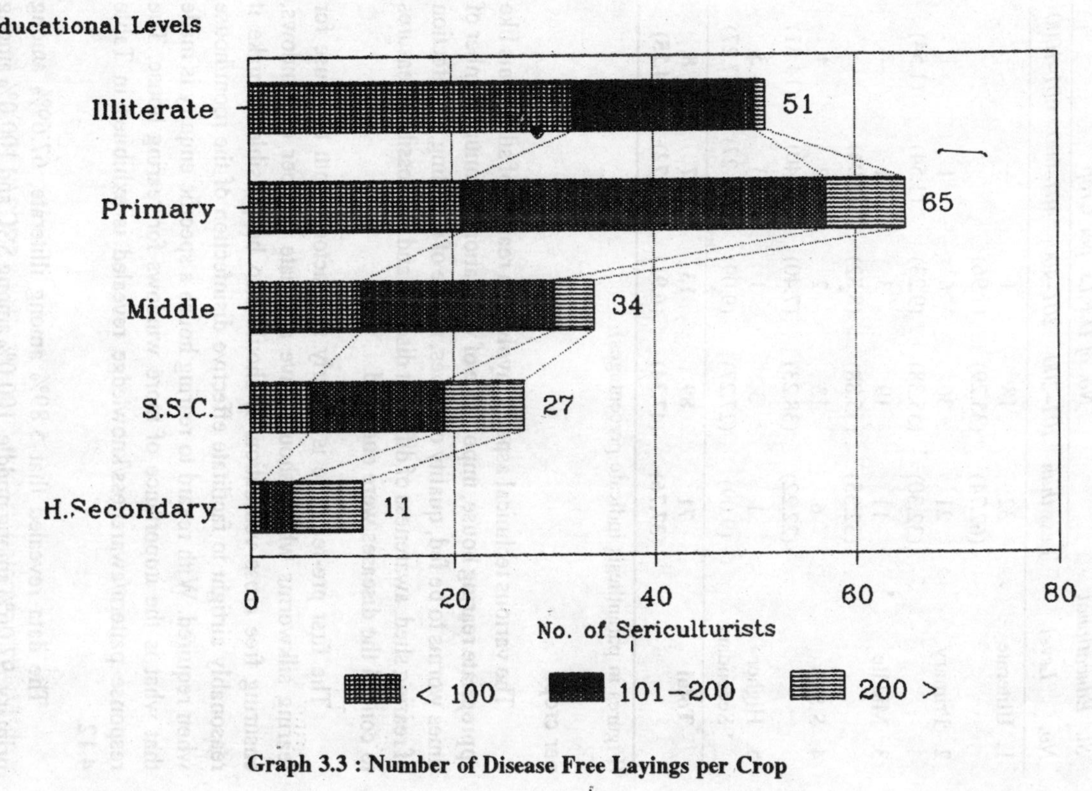

Graph 3.3 : Number of Disease Free Layings per Crop

Table 4.11 : Distribution of Respondents with Number of DFLs per Crop

Sl. No.	Educational Level	No. of D.F.Ls. per Crop				
		Less than	101–200	201–400	401–600	601–1000
1.	Illiterate	32 (62.74)	18 (35.29)	1 (1.96)	---	---
2.	Primary	21 (32.30)	36 (55.38)	6 (9.23)	1 (1.54)	1 (1.54)
3.	Middle	11 (32.35)	19 (55.88)	3 (8.82)	1 (2.94)	---
4.	S.S.C.	6 (22.22)	13 (38.23)	2 (7.40)	2 (7.40)	4 (14.81)
5.	Higher Secondary	1 (9.09)	3 (27.27)	1 (9.09)	3 (27.27)	3 (27.27)
	Total	**71 (37.76)**	**89 (47.34)**	**13 (6.91)**	**7 (3.72)**	**8 (4.25)**

(Figures in paranthesis indicate percentages)

per crop.

The various technical aspects involved in rearing of silkworms like appropriate rearing house, importance of ventilation, optimum number of times worms to be fed, quality of leaves, nature of moulting, disinfection of rearing shed, awareness of different diseases and the possible measures to control the diseases were enquired.

The first pre-requisite is a fairly satisfactory room or house for rearing silkworms which should have adequate number of windows, ensuring free cross ventilation. It should also be possible to make it reasonably airtight to facilitate effective disinfection of the room/house when required. With regard to rearing house a specific enquiry is made that what is the importance of more windows for rearing house. The response pattern/awareness/knowledge revealed is exhibited in Table 4.12.

The data revealed that 5.89% among illiterate, 67.69% among primary, 97.06% among middle, 100.0% among SSC and 100.0% among higher secondary educated farmers gave correct response. The level of knowledge was higher among the educated farmers than illiterate farmers.

The roof of the rearing house should have sufficient high ceiling upto

Table 4.12 : Distribution of Respondents on the Knowledge of More Number of Windows for Rearing House

Sl. No.	*Educational Level*	*Awareness of Correct Response*			
		Correct	*Partly Correct*	*Incorrect*	*Total*
1.	Illiterate	3 (5.89)	9 (17.65)	39 (20.74)	51 (27.13)
2.	Primary	44 (67.69)	14 (21.54)	7 (10.77)	65 (34.57)
3.	Middle	33 (97.06)	1 (2.94)	---	34 (18.05)
4.	Secondary	27 (100.0)	---	---	27 (14.36)
5.	Higher Secondary	11 (100.0)	---	---	11 (5.85)
	Total	**118 (62.76)**	**24 (12.76)**	**46 (24.47)**	**188 (100.0)**

(Figures in paranthesis indicate percentages)

10 feet so that wide fluctions of temperature outside the room do not affect the conditions inside very much. Therefore, the atmospheric temperature and humidity have a bearing on the growth and health of the silkworms. The ideal temperature-humidity conditions under which the silkworms thrive best are 24°C to 27°C and 70% to 90% relative humidity. with regard to environmental requirement the respondents' knowledge is verified through the questions that what should be the ceiling height of rearing house? and what is the rationale behind in that particular height?. The data precipitated for these questions are presented in Table 4.13 and Table 4.14.

The data presented in the Table reveal that out of 51 illiterate farmers 58.82%, 31.37% and 9.80% stated that ceiling height should be in between 6-7, 8-9 and 10-11 feet height respectively. None of the educated farmers stated that the ceiling height should be between 6-7 feet which is incorrect answer except few primary 10.77% educated farmers. The percentage of correct response is higher among educated farmers than the illiterate farmers.

As regards the fact that why it should be of particular height, the data collected is presented in Table 4.14.

Table 4.13 : Distribution of Respondents on the Knowledge of Ceiling Height of Rearing House

Sl. No.	Educational Level	Response of Height in Feet 6–7	8–9	10–11	Total
1.	Illiterate	30 (58.82)	16 (31.37)	5 (9.80)	51 (27.13)
2.	Primary	7 (10.77)	32 (49.23)	26 (40.0)	65 (34.57)
3.	Middle	---	25 (75.53)	9 (26.47)	34 (18.05)
4.	S.S.C.	---	12 (44.44)	15 (55.55)	28 (14.36)
5.	Higher Secondary	---	4 (36.36)	7 (63.64)	11 (5.85)
	Total	**37 (19.68)**	**89 (47.34)**	**62 (32.98)**	**188 (100.0)**

(Figures in paranthesis indicate percentages)

Table 4.14 : Distribution of Respondents on Reason for Particular Height

Sl. No.	Educational Level	Awareness of Correct Response Correct	Partly Correct	Incorrect	Total
1.	Illiterate	3 (5.88)	9 (17.65)	39 (76.47)	51 (27.13)
2.	Primary	39 (60.0)	13 (20.0)	13 (20.0)	65 (34.57)
3.	Middle	32 (94.12)	2 (5.88)	---	34 (18.05)
4.	S.S.C.	27 (100.0)	---	---	27 (14.36)
5.	Higher Secondary	11 (100.0)	---	---	11 (5.85)
	Total	**112 (59.57)**	**24 (12.76)**	**52 (27.66)**	**188 (100.00)**

(Figures in paranthesis indicate percentages)

The data further reveal that educated farmers have the comprehensive knowledge as 60.0% among primary, 94.12% among middle, 100.0% among SSC and 100.0% among higher secondary educated farmers ex-

plained correctly. Among illiterate farmers only 5.88% were aware of rationale behind the particular height of rearing house.

Successful silkworm rearing depends more on technical and managerial manipulations. An enquiry with regard to atmospheric temperature and humidity conditions had been verified with the farmers. The data are presented in Table 4.15.

Table 4.15 : Distribution of Respondents on the Awareness of Ideal Temperature-Humidity Conditions

Sl. No.	*Educational Level*	*Awareness of Correct Response*			*Total*
		Correct	*Partly Correct*	*Incorrect*	
1.	Illiterate	2 (3.92)	24 (47.06)	25 (49.02)	51 (27.13)
2.	Primary	25 (38.46)	27 (41.54)	13 (20.0)	65 (34.57)
3.	Middle	23 (67.65)	11 (32.35)	---	34 (18.05)
4.	S.S.C.	25 (92.59)	2 (7.41)	---	27 (14.36)
5.	Higher Secondary	11 (100.0)	---	---	11 (5.85)
	Total	**86 (45.74)**	**64 (34.04)**	**38 (20.21)**	**188 (100.0)**

(Figures in paranthesis indicate percentages)

The data reveals that 100.0% among higher secondary, 92.59% among SSC, 67.65% among middle, 38.46% among primary and only 3.92% among illiterate farmers were aware of ideal temperature–humidity conditions under which silkworms thrive best.

Ventilation as an element of environmental requirement occupied an important role while rearing silkworms. The young-age worms require higher temperature and humidity and late-age worms, lower temperature and humidy conditions under which the silkworms thrive best. Whether the farmers are aware of this optimum temperate condition and through what mechanism this condition can be achieved is enquired. The analysed data may be seen in Table 4.16.

Table 4.16 : Distribution of Respondents on the Knowledge of Ideal Temperature of Young and Late Age Worms and Importance of Ventilation

Sl. No.	Educational Level	Awareness of Correct Response			
		Correct	Partly Correct	Incorrect	Total
1.	Illiterate	4 (7.84)	29 (56.86)	18 (35.29)	51 (27.13)
2.	Primary	40 (61.54)	20 (30.77)	5 (7.69)	65 (34.57)
3.	Middle	33 (97.06)	1 (2.94)	---	34 (18.05)
4.	S.S.C.	27 (100.0)	---	---	27 (14.36)
5.	Higher Secondary	11 (100.0)	---	---	11 (5.85)
	Total	**115 (61.17)**	**50 (42.37)**	**23 (12.23)**	**188 (100.00)**

(Figures in paranthesis indicate percentages)

The data reveals that 7.84% among illiterate, 61.54% among primary, 97.06% among middle, 100.0% among SSC and 100.0% among higher secondary educated farmers gave the correct answer. Further, they explained that when the day temperature goes very high, all the windows should be kept open during night. This enables the room temperature to come down. Further, all the windows and doors should be opened very early in the morning so that the cooler air from outside is allowed to blow freely inside and bring down the temperature to optimum levels. Thereafter, as the sun rises and the outside temperature goes up, the doors and windows should be closed to keep out the heat and thereby, maintain the rearing room temperature as low as possible. Similarly, during the winter season, the doors and windows should kept closed during nights to keep out the cold and later in the day, as the outside temperature goes up, they should be opened to allow warm air to get in.

The above described manipulations go a long way to provide the near–ideal environmental conditions for the silkworm to grow and thrive well. It is in this context, the need for a suitable rearing room or house conforming to the bare minimum specifications will be found unavoidable.

It was also enquired about how to preserve leaf as fresh a state as possible till they are consumed by the silkworms and spacing of worms in the beds and important aspect to which great care and attention should be given. Those farmers who were educated upto primary and above were able to explain clearly the intricasis of the issues.

Moulting is yet another very critical factor in silkworm rearing that needs to be understood by the farmers very clearly. The silkworm moults four times during its larval growth phase. After attaining the maximum growth in a particular stage or instar, the worm stops feeding, anchors itself to its base and sets about to cast off its existing skin and put on a new skin. The new skin is elastic and permits further growth during the next instar. It is thin and delicate in the beginning and gradually hardens as the worm starts feeding and grows in size. During the moulting period, the worms do not eat. An enquiry with regard to moulting and its special characteristics was done from the farmers. The data collected may be seen in Table 4.17.

Table 4.17 : Distribution of Respondents on the Knowledge of Moulting and Special Characteristics

Sl. No.	*Educational Level*	*Awareness of Correct Response*			
		Correct	*Partly Correct*	*Incorrect*	*Total*
1.	Illiterate	2 (4.08)	9 (17.65)	40 (78.43)	51 (27.13)
2.	Primary	35 (53.85)	15 (23.08)	15 (23.08)	65 (34.57)
3.	Middle	31 (91.18)	3 (8.82)	---	34 (18.05)
4.	S.S.C.	27 (100.0)	---	---	27 (14.36)
5.	Higher Secondary	11 (100.0)	---	---	11 (5.85)
	Total	**106 (56.38)**	**27 (14.36)**	**55 (29.26)**	**188 (100.00)**

(Figures in paranthesis indicate percentages)

The data reveals that 4.08% among illiterate, 53.85% among primary, 91.18% among middle, 100.0% among SSC and 100.0% respondents among higher secondary educated farmers were fully aware of moulting and special characteristics of worms during moulting period.

Further, it was also noticed that the farmers could explain that the worms are made to moult uniformly for ensuring successful crops. As the worms show signs of moulting and as soon as a few worms have settled, attention is paid to the drying of the beds gradually. The paraffin paper used to cover the beds in the early stages should be removed to facilitate drying of the bed. As the bed becomes dry, more and more worms will settle. However, the few worms found still eating, should be continued to be feed with gradually reducing quantities of leaf for the next one or two feeds, by which time almost 100 per cent of worms would settle.

Another important aspect in rearing worms is disinfection of rearing house as well as the appliances used in rearing. They should be invariably disinfected with 2% formalin prior to commencement of every rearing. This will be possible only when there is no overlapping in rearing. It is advisable to take larger rearings, one after the other, rather than having small rearings overlapping one another. Disinfection will prevent possible diseases from the previous silkworm crops through the source of rearing debris present in the rearing house and the rearing appliances. For effective disinfection, the rearing house should be made airtight as far as possible and with the rearing appliances kept inside, the walls, windows, doors and the appliances should be sprayed with 2% formalin solution at the rate of 7-8 litres per 100 sq. metre and the doors closed immediately. After about 24 hours of disinfection, the doors and windows should be opened and the rearing house completely areated atleast 24 hours before commencement of brushing. Almost all respondents revealed that they do disinfect rearing house. And for the remaining part of question the data may be seen in Table 4.18.

The data reveals that 11.76%, 64.61%, 76.47%, 81.48% and 90.91% respondents among illiterate, primary, middle, SSC and higher secondary educated farmers respectively were aware of the percentage of formalin to be used in disinfecting rearing house. None among the category of educated farmers gave incorrect response. This type of knowledge is crucial factor in controlling the spread of diseases effectively.

One of the pre-requisites for effective silkworm rearing is to maintain substantial standards of hygienic conditions to avoid pest and disease outbreak. In silkworm rearing, disease afflictions are rather serious and may occur total loss to the farmers. However, for combating diseases, it could be stated as a general rule that it is easier to prevent the occurrence

Table 4.18 : Distribution of Respondents on the Knowledge of Exact Percentage of Formalin in Disinfection of Rearing House

Sl. No.	*Educational Level*	*Awareness of Correct Response*			*Total*
		Correct	*Partly Correct*	*Incorrect*	
1.	Illiterate	6 (11.76)	26 (50.98)	18 (35.29)	51 (27.13)
2.	Primary	42 (64.61)	23 (35.39)	---	65 (34.57)
3.	Middle	26 (76.47)	8 (23.53)	---	34 (18.05)
4.	S.S.C.	22 (81.48)	5 (18.52)	---	11 (14.36)
5.	Higher Secondary	10 (90.91)	1 (9.09)	---	11 (5.85)
	Total	**106 (56.38)**	**53 (28.19)**	**18 (9.57)**	**188 (100.0)**

(Figures in paranthesis indicate percentages)

of the diseases than trying to cure them when they occur. Therefore, farmers should be well acquint with the nature and symptoms of different diseases. If farmers have the knowledge and skill of identifying diseases carefully, they can adopt controlling measures immediatly. The sampled farmers tested on the knowledge of different seasonal diseases. The data regarding the farmers awareness of different diseases may be seen in Table 4.19 and in Graph 4.4.

It may be seen from the Table 4.19 that none of the illiterate cultivator was aware of all four important diseases. Among the respondents, primary educated farmers 61.54%, middle educated farmers 85.29%, SSC educated farmers 92.59% and higher educated farmers cent percent were aware of all the important seasonal diseases. It can also be deduced from this Table that *awareness about diseases is steadly increasing with the increase in educational level.*

It is important to have a knowledge about the medicine for these diseases along with the knowledge of nature and symptoms of the diseases. This information was ascertained from respondents, analysed and is presented in Table 4.20.

Table 4.19 : Distribution of Respondents on the Knowledge of Different Diseases

(No. of Respondents)

Sl. No.	Educational Level	Pebrine Aware	Pebrine Not aware	Grasserie Aware	Grasserie Not aware	Flacherie Aware	Flacherie Not aware	Ugi Aware	Ugi Not aware	All Aware	All Not aware	Total Respon-dents
1.	Illiterate	13 (25.49)	38 (74.51)	2 (3.92)	49 (96.08)	--	51 (100.0)	36 (70.59)	15 (29.41)	--	51 (100.0)	51 (100.0)
2.	Primary	40 (61.54)	25 (38.46)	22 (33.85)	43 (66.15)	20 (30.77)	45 (69.23)	60 (92.31)	5 (7.69)	40 (61.54)	15 (23.08)	65 (34.57)
3.	Middle	30 (88.24)	4 (11.76)	27 (79.41)	7 (20.59)	25 (73.53)	9 (26.47)	34 (100.0)	--	29 (85.29)	5 (14.71)	34 (18.06)
4.	S.S.C.	27 (100.0)	---	25 (92.59)	2 (7.41)	24 (88.88)	3 (11.12)	27 (100.0)	---	25 (92.59)	2 (7.41)	27 (14.36)
5.	Higher Secondary	11 (100.0	---	11 (100.0)	---	11 (100.0)	---	11 (100.0)	---	11 (100.0)	---	11 (100.0)
	Total	**121 (64.36)**	**67 (35.64)**	**87 (46.28)**	**101 (53.72)**	**80 (42.53)**	**108 (57.45)**	**168 (89.36)**	**20 (10.64)**	**105 (55.85)**	**73 (38.83)**	**188 (100.0)**

(Figures in paranthesis indicate percentages)

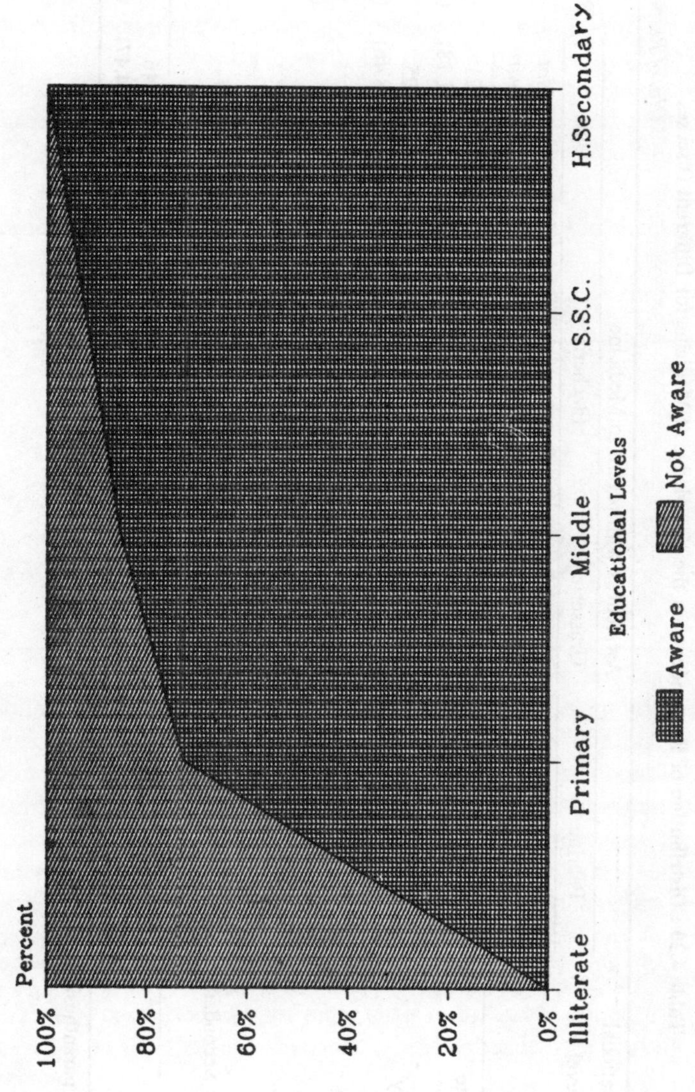

Graph 4.4 : Knowledge of Different Diseases

Table 4.20 : Distribution of Respondents on the Knowledge of Medicine for Different Diseases

(No. of Respondents)

Sl. No.	Educational Level	Awareness with regard to Medicine								Total Respon-dents
		Pebrine		Grasserie		Flacherie		Ugi		
		Aware	*Not aware*	*Aware*	*Not aware*	*Aware*	*Not aware*	*Aware*	*Not aware*	
1.	Illiterate	4 (7.84)	47 (92.16)	---	51 (100.0)	51 (100.0)	---	30 (58.82)	21 (41.18)	51 (100.0)
2.	Primary	25 (38.46)	40 (61.54)	12 (18.46)	53 (81.54)	10 (15.38)	55 (84.62)	40 (61.54)	25 (38.46)	65 (34.57)
3.	Middle	22 (88.24)	12 (11.76)	15 (79.41)	19 (20.59)	19 (73.53)	15 (26.47)	34 (100.0)	---	34 (18.06)
4.	S.S.C.	25 (92.59)	2 (7.41)	24 (92.59)	3 (7.41)	26 (88.88)	1 (11.12)	27 (100.0)	---	27 (14.36)
5.	Higher Secondary	11 (100.0	---	11 (100.0)	---	11 (100.0)	---	11 (100.0)	---	11 (5.85)
	Total	**87 (46.28)**	**101 (53.72)**	**62 (32.98)**	**126 (67.02)**	**66 (35.11)**	**122 (64.89)**	**142 (75.53)**	**46 (24.47)**	**188 (100.0)**

(Figures in paranthesis indicate percentages)

Based on the data presented in Table 4.20 farmers who are educated upto higher secondary, cent percent were aware of the medicines for all important seasonal diseases. Thus, farmers who are educated can be a better managers in crisis rather than illiterates. It was also found that there is a strong association between the variables since its r value = .3127.

Education generally has the effect of lowering the marginal costs of acquiring production related information and of raising the marginal benefits of such information. Such lowering of marginal costs may occur for a variety of reasons, including the improved communication skills of more educated persons, and the possible superiority of their contacts with elite people. In the realm of sericulture, upgradation of existing technology as well as new technology being introduced constantly. Those who can decode the information will benefit. Cocoon market prices change drastically within a short span of time. Who can cope up with this situation? Those who can foresee and comprehend the existing technology can be fitest, and shall survive and prosper in this field. A specific enquiry was made regarding market price, and other related information. The data may be seen in Table 4.21.

Table 4.21 : Distribution of Respondents on How do they Manage Information Including Market Price

Sl. No.	*Educational Level*	*Response Pattern* Follow neibour farmer	Literatue like manuals pamphlets and leaflets	Direct access to department officials	*Total*
1.	Illiterate	48	3	--	51
		(94.12)	(5.88)		(27.13)
2.	Primary	3	61	1	65
		(4.62)	(93.85)	(1.54)	(34.57)
3.	Middle	1	32	1	34
		(2.94)	(94.12)	(2.94)	(18.09)
4.	S.S.C.	---	23	4	27
			(85.19)	(14.81)	(14.36)
5.	Higher Secondary	---	5	6	11
			(45.45)	(54.55)	(5.85)
	Total	**52**	**124**	**12**	**188**
		(27.66)	**(65.96)**	**(6.38)**	**(100.0)**

(Figures in paranthesis indicate percentages)

It is revealed from the Table 4.21 that the dependency on neighbouring farmers was as high as 94.12% among illiterates. Direct link with information network existed and gradually increased among the educated farmers. Thus, schooling is increased the rate of acquisition of useful information and such an increase in information–acquisition was constituted a major source for productive efficiency among educated producers.

The ultimate aim of any producer is to get more production–more income. In the earlier paras of this chapter, I have analysed different variables which are to be manipulated/manage carefully. All such varriables established that there is a positive correlation with education variable. The data with regard to crop-wise cocoon production per annum has been collected from farmers and computed the productivity per 100 disease free layings. The analysed data may be seen in Table 4.22 and in Graph 4.5.

Table 4.22 : Distribution of Respondents on Productivity of Cocoons per 100 dfls.

Sl. No.	*Educational Level*	*Cocoon Productivity for 100 dfls.*			
		10–20 kgs.	*21–40 kgs.*	*41–50 kgs.*	*Total*
1.	Illiterate	30 (58.82)	21 (41.18)	---	51 (27.13)
2.	Primary	---	52 (80.0)	13 (20.0)	65 (34.57)
3.	Middle	---	29 (85.29)	5 (14.71)	34 (18.09)
4.	S.S.C.	---	16 (59.26)	11 (40.74)	27 (14.36)
5.	Higher Secondary	---	3 (27.27)	8 (72.73)	11 (5.85)
	Total	**30 (15.96)**	**111 (59.04)**	**37 (19.68)**	**188 (100.0)**

(Figures in paranthesis indicate percentages)

It may be seen from the Table 4.22 that 58.82% of illiterate farmers had produced in the lowest range of 10–20 kgs cocoon Productivity per 100 dfls. 41.18% among illiterate, 80.0% among Primary, 85.29% among middle, 59.26% among SSC and 27.27% among higher secondary educated farmers had produced in the range of 21–40 Kgs per 100 dfls. The data proved that the highest cocoon productivity 41–50 kgs is achieved by

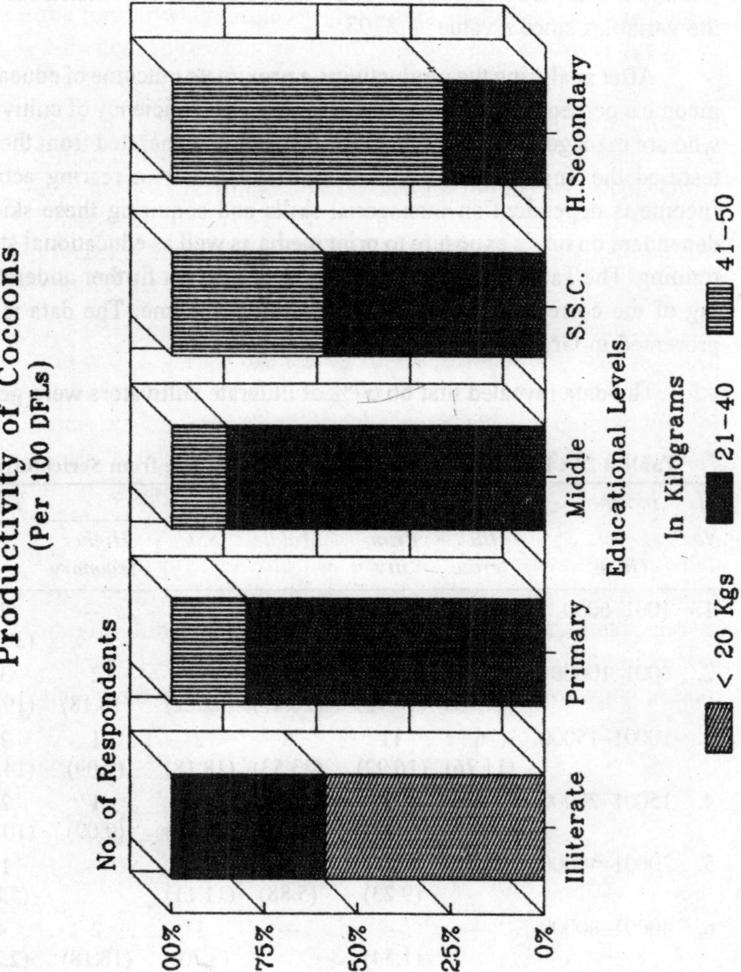
GRAPH - 4.5
Productivity of Cocoons
(Per 100 DFLs)
No. of Respondents
100%
75%
50%
25%
0%
Illiterate
Primary
Middle
S.S.C.
H.Secondary
Educational Levels
In Kilograms
< 20 Kgs
21–40
41–50

educated farmers. The productivity of the farmers proved that their education played a very crucial role in management/manipulate the cocoon rearing. It was also found that strong positive correlation existed between the variables since *r* value = .2703.

After analysing the productivity, a proximate outcome of education, income a perceptible variable, is measured as the efficiency of cultivators who are managers of the activity. The Table 4.23 generated from the data testified the importance of educational component in rearing activity. Income is dependent on managerial skills and acquiring these skills is dependent on one's exposure to print media as well as educational status/ training. The Table 4.23 given below is presented for further understanding of the correlation between education and income. The data is also presented in Graph 4.6.

The data revealed that 66.67% of illiterate cultivators were getting

Table 4.23 : Distribution of Respondents on Income from Sericulture

Sl. No.	*Income Level (Rs.)*	*Educational Level*					*Total*
		Illi-terate	*Prim-ary*	*Middle*	*SSC*	*Higher Seconary*	
1.	1001–6000	34 (66.67)	30 (46.15)	10 (29.41)	1 (3.70)	---	75 (39.89)
2.	6001–10000	9 (17.65)	11 (16.92)	9 (26.47)	6 (22.22)	2 (18.18)	37 (19.68)
3.	10001–15000	6 (11.76)	11 (16.92)	8 (23.53)	2 (18.18)	1 (9.09)	28 (14.89)
4.	15001–20000	2 (3.92)	5 (7.69)	3 (8.82)	9 (33.33)	1 (9.09)	20 (10.64
5.	20001–40000	---	6 (9.23)	2 (5.88)	3 (11.11)	---	11 (5.85)
6.	40001–80000	---	--- (1.54)	---	1 (3.70)	2 (18.18)	4 (2.13)
7.	80001–100000	---	---	---	1 (3.70)	2 (18.18)	3 (1.60)
8.	1 Lakh & above	---	1 (1.54)	2 (5.88)	4 (14.81)	3 (27.27)	10 (5.32)
	Total	**51 (27.13)**	**65 (34.57)**	**34 (18.09)**	**27 (14.36)**	**11 (5.85)**	**188 (100.00)**

(Figures in paranthesis indicate percentages)

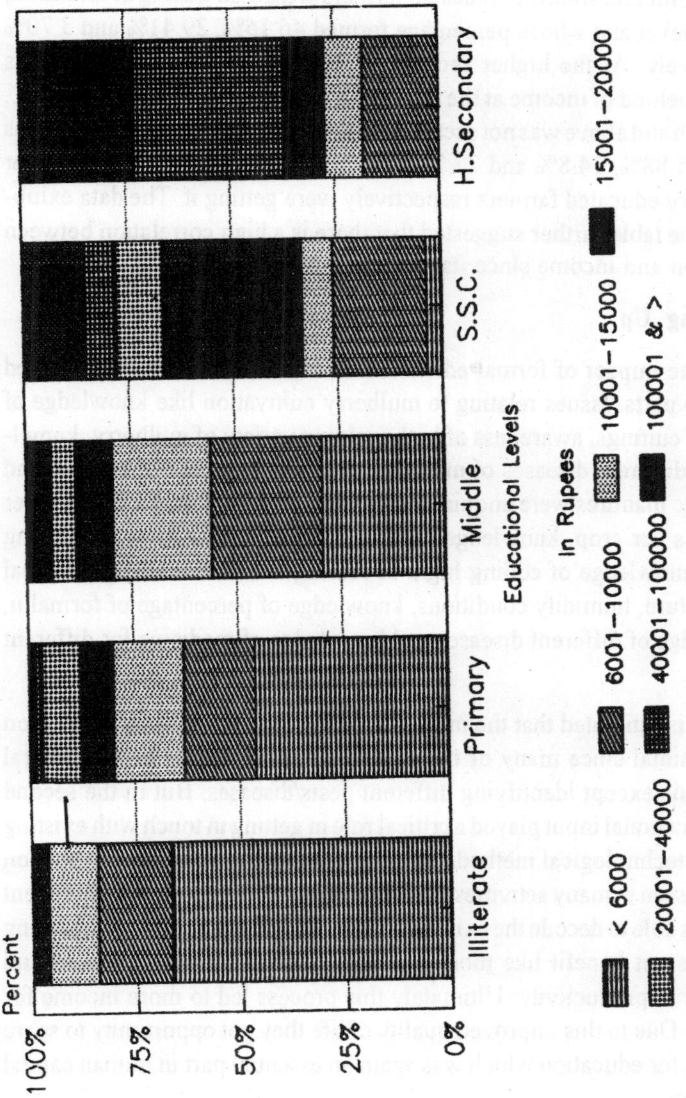

Graph 4.6 : Income Distribution

Rs. 6000/- annual income which is at the minimum level. Whereas few primary, middle and SSC educated farmers were also getting at minimum income level and whose percentage formed 46.15%, 29.41% and 3.70% respectively. At the higher secondary level none of the cultivator was trailing behind of income at the minimum level. Highest income level i.e., Rs. 1 lakh and above was not accruing to any of the illiterate farmer whereas 1.54%, 5.88%, 14.8% and 27.27% of primary, middle, SSC and higher secondary educated farmers respectively were getting it. The data exhibited in the table further suggested that there is a high correlation between education and income since its r value = .6230.

Summing Up

The impact of formal education on Sericulturists broadly divided into two parts. Issues relating to mulberry cultivation like knowledge of depth of cuttings, awareness of high yielding variety of mulberry, knowledge of different diseases of mulberry plantation and use of organic and inorganic manures were enquired in the first part. And issues like number of DFL's per crop, knowledge of more number of windows for rearing house, knowledge of ceiling hight of rearing house, knowledge of ideal temperature, humidity conditions, knowledge of percentage of formalin, knowledge of different diseases and knowledge of medicine for different diseases.

It is estimated that the impact of education on mulberry cultivation was minimal since many of the operations were similar to agricultural operations except identifying different pests/diseases. But in the second part educational input played a critical role in getting in touch with existing modern technological methods through print media. Impact of education has also seen in many activities in cocoon rearing. The educated respondent who was able to decode the existing information and make use of in rearing practices got benefit like more produce, large quantity of cocoons and increase in productivity. Ultimately this process led to more income for farmers. Due to this improved quality of life they got opportunity to spare children for education which was again an essential part in human capital formation.

Therefore, one of the objective of the study set for enquiry is greatly accomplished as the findings reveal that there is a positive association and significant correlation between education and the management of sericultural activities.

References

1. Smith, T.L–*Sociology of Rural Life*, Harper, New York, 1947.
2. Shultz, T.W–"Capital Formation by Education", *Journal of Political Economy*, December, 1960.
3. Scribner, Syliva and Michael Cole–The Psychology of Literature, Massachusetts, Harvard University Press, Cambridge, 1981.
4. Jamison, Dean and Peter, Mock–"Farmer Education and Farm Efficiency in Nepal: The Role of Schooling, Extension Services and Cognitive Skills", *World Development*, No.12, 1984.
5. Cotlear, Daniel–"Farmer Education and Farm Efficiency in Peru: The Role of Schooling, Extension Services and Migration", EDT Discussion Paper 49, *World Bank*, Washington D.C, 1986.
6. Krishna Swamy, S–*New Technology of Silkworm Rearing*, Central Silk Board (Repirnted from the Bulletin No.2 of the SR & TI, Mysore) Bangalore, 1990.
7. ———, *New Technology of Silkworm Rearing*, Central Silk Board (Reprinted from the Bulletin No.2 of the SR & TI, Mysore) Bangalore, 1990.

5

EDUCATION AND SOCIAL DEVELOPMENT

> *"Education is not mere acquisition of information but the expansion of natural powers, it is the attainment of fullest natural growth of the individual".*
>
> —Rousseau

Hardly anything in our midst is static. Everything changes, every organism grows, every life flows. The society composed of human beings also undergoes changes. These changes occur in its cultural pattern, in its structure and consequently on its members. This process of change is quite complicated and needs a careful and deep understanding.

Education is considered as the most powerful instrument of social change. It is through education that the society can bring desirable changes and modernize itself. Education is the most important prime mover for not only economic development but also bring social change. The knowledge, skills and values acquired through education, not only meet the economic needs of society, but they are also permeated with a social content.

Education, no doubt, can help the process of social changes as a necessary and vitally important collateral factor. It can help to stimulate, accelerate and work out that process by disseminating and inculcating knowledge, information, skills and values appropriate to the changing socio-economic issues. Education may help the process of far-reaching social change by using its *liberating* and *rebelatory* role by examining and analysing the existing social situation, by contraposing an alternative ideology to the established one.

The relation between education and social change has been examined in rural contexts, where rigid class systems have proved barriers to education as well as agricultural changes. Holmberg[1] and Dobyns[2] Jointly as well as separately reported the vicos action research project. The project was a study of the role of enlightenment in social development.

"In the above project an attempt was made to transform a stagnant peruvian hacienda inhabited by subsistence farmers into a modernizing community with institutions incorporating participant values". The findings of this project were that "education became enmeshed in wider social change as knowledge became the means to status and effective participation". It was also found that the most modernized citizens in the emergent community were youngsters who had attended school. This project has clearly established the importance of education in modernizing a community.

In another study by Lerner[3] also was found that the key to modernization lies in the participant society, that is, one in which people go through school, read news papers, are in the wage and market economy, participate politically through elections and change opinions on matters to note that literacy not only proved to be key variable in moving from a traditional to a transitional society but also the pivotal agent in the transition to a fully participant society.

The study of Philip Foster[4] in Ghana and Shils[5] in India have also revealed the role of education in social change. Foster came to the conclusion that it was formal western schooling in Ghana that created a cultural environment in which innovations could take place. Shils making a study of the intellectuals in India came to the conclusion that if there is to be any successful bridge of the gap between traditional and modern societies, it is the western educated intellectuals who must perform the task.

India present a typical example among the underdeveloped nations. It has the lowest per capita income and a mass of illiterate population. Its population growth rate is tremendous while the economic growth is slow and erratic. Yet whole of the nation is not backward. Quite an apppreciable chunk of its population is well set on the road to modernization. There is however, a mass of people who are traditional oriented. There is thus a situation in this country in which modernity and traditionalism are in a typical mixture. It is difficult to understand how modernization can take place unless a hatred towards those cultural patterns is not created which are decadent and fossilised. For example, unless religious bigotry is banished or a hatred towards it is created, the ideals of secular culture cannot be promoted.

Therefore, education is considered to be the main instrument of change in social sphere as well. Here change was visualised in the framework of the tradition–modernity paradigm, with stress on the cultural rather than on the structural change. By and large even within the village variety of changes are taking place like economic change, social change and political change. It is very difficult to estimate the social change or non-economic change of education.

The aim of this chapter is to understand the influence of education on social issues like change in values, beliefs, attitudes and modernization among sericulturists. The source for this chapter is empirical data collected from the selected respondents as well as my personal observation. The foregoing text will examine the changes in issues like (i) modernization in values and beliefs, (ii) demographic aspects, (iii) health and nutritional issues, (iv) social mobility, (v) social relations, (vi) decision making process and (vii) empowerment of women.

Modernization in Values and Beliefs

Education has an interdependent relation with other modernization variables but modernization, as it develops, also impels literacy forward. The arrows expressing this relationship are reciprocal as seen in the diagram–5.1.

A small increase in one variable probably leads to a minute increment in the other which in turn leads to change in the first variable, and so forth.

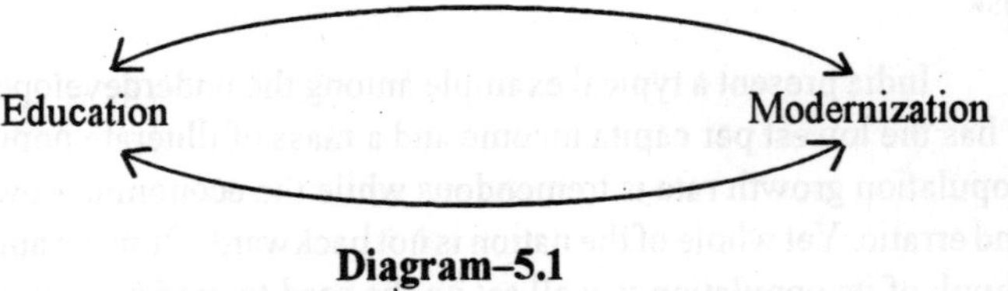

Diagram–5.1

The process of modernization among sericulturists will be examined in this chapter. The reference point for the process of modernization is respondents thinking/behavioural pattern. The inherent inequlity in terms of sex, caste and age is beyond one's capacity to control; but the inequalities pertaining to the concept of purity–pollution, status consciousness etc., have been reduced among the educated sericulturists. Very often new technologies are introduced by Department of Sericulture (DOS) in the realm of rearing practices. Sericulturists, cutting across the social barriers used to discuss the viability and feasibility of new technologies near the rearing sheds or near the common place where they use to meet regularly. Visiting to others rearing sheds and trying to give suggestions as well learn new techniques is a common scene. In this process of reciprocity and give and take attitude is taking place not withstanding to social difference and descrimination. Hence, broadly modernization is taking place among sericulturists which is a positive sign for economic development also.

Impact of education among respondents has been analysed in terms of changes in beliefs and values which play a critical role in the development of individual and society. Exposure to modern education and mass media made the societies transform from traditional to modernity. Sericulturists while cultivating mulberry as well as cocoon rearing observe many customs and traditions. A woman in her menstruation period should not enter into the rearing house and a pregnant woman is not allowed to feed the worms etc. It is very common to see breaking a coconut and waiting for an auspicious day to start prepare Chawki inspite of the leaves turning into yellow colour in the mulberry garden. Some farmers are ignorent about the correct percentage of formalin solution to be used while disinfection of rearing house but very particular about performing the puja (worship) before starting the rearing. Like this there are innumerable sentiments and beliefs prevalent in the minds of farmers. An opinion question with regard to these beliefs and values was canvassed among the sampled respondents. The analysed data is presented in Table 5.1.

The impact of education on the respondents beliefs and values with regard to pregnancy, child birth and menstruation is inversely correlated. There are 74.51% of illiterate, 10.77% of primary educated, 5.88% of middle educated and 3.70% of SSC educated respondents who believe as well as practice these values. The percentage of respondents who believe in these beliefs and values gradually decreases as the educational status

Table 5.1 : Distribution of Respondent's Opinion about their Beliefs and Values

Sl. No.	*Educational Level*	*Response Pattern*			
		No belief/ no practice	*Belief/ practice*	*Believe but not practice*	*Total*
1.	Illiterate	5 (9.80)	38 (74.51)	8 (15.69)	51 (27.13)
2.	Primary	54 (83.08)	7 (10.77)	4 (6.15)	65 (34.74)
3.	Middle	32 (94.12)	2 (5.88)	---	34 (18.09)
4.	SSC	26 (96.30)	1 (3.70)	---	27 (14.36)
5.	Higher Secondary	11 (100.0)	---	---	11 (5.85)
	Total	**128 (69.09)**	**48 (25.53)**	**12 (6.38)**	**188 (100.0)**

(Figures in Paranthesis indicate percentages).

among respondents increases. Education played a decisive role in inculcating positive thinking in modernizing beliefs and values.

Demographic Aspects

Theodore Schultz[6] has pointed out that with economic development and the requirement for highly educated and trained manpower, parents become increasingly concerned with the quality of their children, as against the number of children emphasised in traditional societies.

For proper upbringing of children it is necessary that they should be given proper food, clothing, education etc., which necessitates parents to make earnest efforts to limit the number of their children. The rapid decline of mortality in Kerala was the outcome of the spread of education. It also appears that the rate of acceptance of contraceptives is crucially dependent on the level of infant mortality and on the literacy rate. What may be more important is a higher average rate of literacy of the whole population. Therefore, investment in a growth agent like education has the twin advantages of stimulating the process of development and lowering fertility, accelerating the process of development.

This phenomenon was examined among sericulturists. Many educated sericulturists formed positive opinion about the small family norm. In addition to positive attitude towards small family norm, farmers were having knowledge about the different birth control methods. Specific enquiry was made about the opinion regarding small family norm and its importance. The response pattern is presented in Table 5.2.

Table 5.2 : Distribution of Respondents' Opinion about the Small Family Norm

Sl. No.	*Educational Level*	*Response Pattern*			*Total*
		Agree	*Disagree*	*Can't say*	
1.	Illiterate	24 (47.06)	22 (43.14)	5 (9.80)	51 (27.13)
2.	Primary	48 (73.85)	15 (23.08)	2 (3.08)	65 (34.74)
3.	Middle	33 (97.06)	1 (2.94)	---	34 (18.09)
4.	SSC	27 (100.0)	---	---	27 (14.36)
5.	Higher Secondary	11 (100.0)	---	---	11 (5.85)
	Total	**143 (76.06)**	**38 (20.21)**	**7 (3.72)**	**188 (100.0)**

(Figures in Paranthesis indicate percentages).

The data revealed that 76.06% of respondents appreciated the importance of small family norm and about 20.21% of respondents disagreed about its importance. In addition to this dimension, data were also analysed on respondents educational levels. It was revealed that 73.85% of primary, 97.06% of middle, 100.0% of SSC as well as higher secondary educated farmers understood the importance of small family norm. At the same time 43.14% of illiterate farmers did not appreciate the importance of small family norm and its role in ecomomic development.

Health and Nutritional Issues

Health and Nutritional levels are the indicators of any development process. Improvement in quality of life is the prime concern for any development project. The term quality of life connotes the improvement in health and nutritional level of people, improvement in shelter and access to social services. In the households where income increased due to the efficiency in management of sericultural activities, the quality of life has improved drastically. Data regarding the consumption level and pattern are not dealt with in detail but the personal observation corroborated this finding. An opinion question was canvassed among the respondnents for eliciting data on this issue. The analysed data is presented in Table 5.3.

Table 5.3 : Table Showing the Distribution of Respondents Opinion on Quality of Life

Sl. No.	*Educational Level*	*Type of Opinion* Changed Drastically	Changed Moderately	No Change	*Total*
1.	Illiterate	7 (9.59)	50 (68.49)	16 (21.92)	73 (33.18)
2.	Primary	23 (31.51)	38 (52.05)	12 (16.44)	73 (33.18)
3.	Middle	16 (44.44)	20 (55.56)	---	36 (16.36)
4.	SSC	21 (77.78)	6 (22.22)	---	27 (12.27)
5.	Higher Secondary	11 (100.0)	---	---	11 (5.0)
	Total	**78 (35.45)**	**144 (51.82)**	**28 (12.73)**	**220 (100.0)**

(Figures in Paranthesis indicate percentages).

It can be observed from the Table that 100.0% among higher secondary, 77.78% among SSC, 44.44% among middle and 31.51% among primary educated respondents revealed that there has been improvement in the quality of life. However, 21.92% among illiterate and 16.44% among primary educated respondents opinied that there has been no change in their quality life.

Social Mobility

Mobility denotes movement or the capacity to move. The term social mobility refers to the process by which individuals move from one social position to that of the other. There are two principal types of social mobility (i) *Horizontal* and (ii) *Verticle*. Horizontal social mobility refers to the transition of the individuals from one social group to that of the other situated at the same level. For example, a manual worker becoming rickshaw puller is an example of horizontal occupational mobility. In this type of mobility shift takes place without any distinct transformation of the social status of an individual or social group in the vertical direction. The vertical social mobility refers to transition of an individual that results in a shift from one social position to another. Vertical social mobility takes place in two different directions (i) *Upward* and (ii) *Downward.* The upward social mobility takes place when an individual of lower social strata moves to a higher social status, whereas downward social mobility results in dropping of individuals from higher social status to that of lower without causing any damage to the prestige of their original group.

Social mobility results due to a number of factors. Some of them are (i) the level of formal education (ii) an individual's class position, namely the economic status (iii) caste background and (iv) migration. By and large education is the major means through which people are able to improve their overall position in society.

The phenomenon of social mobility was observed among the sampled respondents. The horizontal social mobility has taken place more among the scheduled caste and backward class respondents. Marginal and small farmers who belonged to SC and BC communities used to depend on agricultural wages before taking up sericulture. Education helped the farmers to take up the modern activity and increased their household earnings. Among many households of these communities had reduced their dependency on agriculture labour market. Now the status has changed from agricultural wage earners to sericulturists.

When enquired about whether farmers would like to keep the children in the same occupation or will they allow them to adopt new occupation and send them to school. Many respondents offered the view that they prefer to send their children for education. To strengthen my point, the enrolment pattern in the study area was collected. Education of the children especially of poor, backward and the hitherto neglected is a dynamic force making for positive social change. A school is a symbol of hope whose effect upon the world community should never be underestimate. Big farmers belonging to higher castes are sending their children to residential convents and English medium schools. The data collected from the existing primary and high schools at Maluguru is presented in Table 5.4 and 5.5 respectively:

Table 5.4 : Respondent's Children Educational Status (upto Primary Level) at Maluguru Village

Sl. No.	*Academic Standard*	*Different Academic Years and Sex-wise Enrollment*												*Total*
		1989–90			1990–91			1991–92			1992–93			
		M	*F*	*T*	*M*	*F*	*T*	*M*	*F*	*T*	*M*	*F*	*T*	
1.	1st	32	21	53 (36.30)	30	27	57 (35.40)	35	29	64 (39.02)	32	31	63 (36.21)	237 (36.74)
2.	2nd	26	15	41 (28.08)	25	13	38 (22.60)	12	16	28 (17.07)	22	18	40 (22.99)	147 (22.79)
3.	3rd	13	4	17 (11.64)	17	10	27 (16.77)	19	11	30 (18.29)	10	9	19 (10.92)	93 (14.42)
4.	4th	16	5	21 (14.38)	13	3	16 (9.94)	15	8	23 (14.02)	19	9	28 (16.09)	88 (13.64)
5.	5th	10	4	14 (9.59)	16	7	23 (14.29)	17	2	19 (11.58)	16	8	24 (13.79)	80 (12.40)
	Total	**97**	**49**	**146** (22.63)	**101**	**60**	**161** (24.96)	**98**	**66**	**164** (25.43)	**99**	**75**	**174** (26.98)	**645** (100.0)

M = Male F = Female T = Total

Source : Mandal Praja Parishad Primary School, Maluguru

(Figures in Parenthesis indicate percentages)

Table 5.5 : Respondents' Children Educational Status (upto High School) at Maluguru Village

Sl. No.	*Academic Standard*	*Different Academic Years and Sex-wise Enrollment*												*Total*
		1989–90			1990–91			1991–92			1992–93			
		M	*F*	*T*	*M*	*F*	*T*	*M*	*F*	*T*	*M*	*F*	*T*	
1.	VI	24	6	30 (16.76)	36	6	42 (23.08)	58	12	70 (33.98)	48	9	57 (27.14)	199 (25.61)
2.	VII	45	13	58 (32.40)	30	12	42 (23.08)	37	7	44 (21.36)	51	10	61 (29.05)	205 (26.38)
3.	VIII	35	6	41 (22.91)	32	12	44 (24.18)	24	7	31 (15.05)	25	7	32 (15.24)	148 (19.05)
4.	IX	27	3	30 (16.76)	25	6	31 (17.03)	27	12	39 (18.93)	19	11	30 (14.29)	130 (16.73)
5.	X	17	3	20 (11.17)	19	4	23 (12.64)	15	7	22 (10.68)	18	12	30 (14.29)	95 (12.23)
	Total	**148**	**33**	**179 (23.04)**	**142**	**40**	**182 (23.42)**	**161**	**45**	**206 (26.51)**	**161**	**49**	**210 (27.03)**	**777 (100.0)**

M = Male F = Female T = Total

Source : Zilla Praja Parishad High School, Maluguru

(Figures in Parenthesis indicate percentages)

It is evident from the Table 5.4 that enrolment pattern for the last four years has given a strong support to the stand that the farmers recognised the impcrtance of education. The percentage of enrolment has increased from year after year at the aggregate level. The cumulative percentage or enrolment also has steadily increased from 22.63% during 1989–90, 24.96% during 1990–91, 25.43% during 1991–92 and to 26.98% during 1992–93.

The data presented in the Table 5.5 reiterate the statement that the farmers realised the importance of education. The percentage of enrolment has increased gradually from 1989–90 to 1992–93.

The same set of data was also collected from the village Tumakunta where 50 respondents are drawn in which 18 are cultivators and remaining 32 are non-cultivators of mulberry. The analysed data is presented in Table 5.6.

It can be seen from the Table that the enrolment pattern in Tumakunta is more or less stagnant. For this, the reasons attributed by the respondents are (i) low literacy level (ii) dependence on agricultural wages and (iii) low level of aspirations among the respondents.

Thus, it can be concluded that education has potentiality of initiating social mobility among sericulturists, as well as to pave the inter-generational social mobility that the sample households have been witnessing. Particularly, education should become still more useful and a leverage of social uplift among the scheduled caste and backward class sections.

Social Relations

Marion Levy[7] has indicated that the aspects of social relations of people may be discussed in terms of (i) rationality and traditionalism, (ii) Universalism and particularism, (iii) functional specificity and functional diffuseness and (iv) avoidence and intimacy. As the level of modernization of a society increases, the emphasis on explaining one's reason for doing a given thing in scientifically defensible terms.

The concept of modernization in social relations among respondents is verified based on a opinion enquiry. Practice of discrimination and untouchability is common phenomenon even today in some rural areas. Due to the spread of education and impact of industrialization the problem of untouchability and other related purity–pollution concepts have dras-

Table 5.6 : Respondents' Children Educational Status (Primary Level) at Tumakunta

Sl. No.	*Academic Standard*	*Different Academic Years and Sex-wise Enrollment*												*Total*
		1989–90			1990–91			1991–92			1992–93			
		M	*F*	*T*	*M*	*F*	*T*	*M*	*F*	*T*	*M*	*F*	*T*	
1.	1st	32	26	58 (32.77)	28	20	48 (31.37)	34	16	50 (31.06)	35	14	49 (30.63)	205 (31.49)
2.	2nd	27	14	41 (23.16)	22	10	32 (20.92)	16	15	31 (19.25)	16	14	30 (18.75)	134 (20.58)
3.	3rd	12	11	23 (12.99)	24	10	34 (22.22)	25	9	34 (21.12)	22	10	32 (20.0)	123 (18.89)
4.	4th	24	4	28 (15.82)	12	7	19 (12.42)	19	9	28 (17.39)	20	9	29 (18.13)	104 (15.98)
5.	5th	11	16	27 (15.25)	18	2	20 (13.07)	13	5	18 (11.18)	18	2	20 (12.50)	85 (13.06)
	Total	**106**	**71**	**177 (27.19)**	**104**	**49**	**153 (23.50)**	**107**	**54**	**161 (24.73)**	**111**	**49**	**160 (24.58)**	**651 (100.0)**

M = Male F = Female T = Total

Source : Mandal Praja Parishad Primary School, Tumakunta

(Figures in Parenthesis indicate percentages)

tically reduced. The main factors responsible for modern thinking are (i) rationalization of traditional values, (ii) recognition of human dignity and (iii) change in thinking pattern. All these modern values emerged and developed due to the spread of education. To support the theoretical concept of modernization in social relations, empirical data has been collected in the form of respondents opinion. The analysed data is presented in Table 5.7 and in Graph 5.1.

Table 5.7 : Table Showing the Distribution of Respondents on their Opinion regarding Untouchability and Discrimination

Sl. No.	*Educational Level*	*Response Pattern*		*Total*
		Believe & Practice	*No Belief &* No Practice	
1.	Illiterate	41 (80.39)	10 (19.61)	51 (27.13)
2.	Primary	15 (23.08)	50 (76.92)	65 (34.57)
3.	Middle	5 (14.71)	29 (85.29)	34 (18.09)
4.	SSC	---	27 (100.0)	27 (14.36)
5.	Higher Secondary	---	11 (100.0)	11 (5.85)
	Total	**61 (32.45)**	**127 (67.55)**	**188 (100.0)**

(Figures in Paranthesis indicate percentages).

It is noted from the Table that 32.45% of respondents believe and practice and 67.55% of respondents have no belief and do not practice untouchability. The similar set of data is analysed on respondents educational level. The belief and practice is very strong as 80.39% of illiterate respondents stated that they believe and practice. As the educational level is increasing, the percentage of believers and practitioners are decreasing.

This fact is also testified with my personal observation, when few of twice born status respondents who were rearing worms in rented sheds, belonging to the scheduled caste community, without any inhibition they used to go to scheduled caste basti and rear their worms. Neighbours (mostly small and marginal scheduled caste farmers) used to visit the sheds

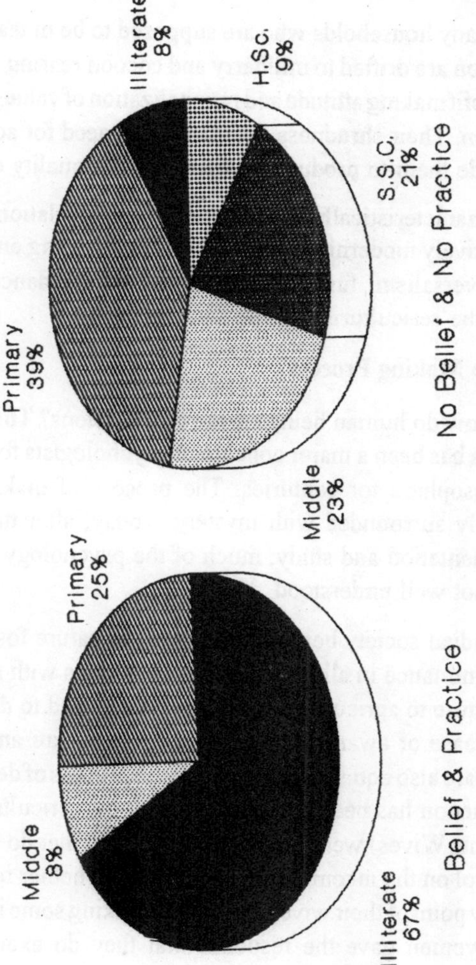

Graph 5.2 : Opinion on Untouchability and Discrimination

and try to make a suggestion. In this process the reciprocity and interaction used to take place cutting across the caste barriers. This may be stray case but this lends support to the fact ҆hat caste restrictions are declining.

Many households who are supposed to be in teaching and business profession are drifted to mulberry and cocoon rearing activity in the study area. Profit making attitude and rationalization of values developed through education. Their shrudness, hardwork and need for achievement motivation made them to produce best and highest quality of cocoons.

Characteristically, the structure of social relations among sericulturists relatively modernized and reflect on increasing emphasis on rationality, Universalism, functional neutrality or avoidance. This has proved among the sericulturists in the study area.

Decision Making Process

How do human beings make the decisions? This seemingly simple question has been a major concern of psychologists for many decades and of philosophers for centuries. The process of making a decision was inevitably surrounded with mystery. Today, after much theorizing and experimentation and study, much of the psychology of decision making is still not well understood.

Indian society being patriarchical in nature fostered the culture of male dominance in all the activities. Decisions with regard to household expenditure to agricultural operations male used to dominate. But due to the increase of awareness, mass media exposure and education among women are also equally taking part in the process of decision making. This phenomenon has been examined among the sericulturists. Women (Respondents Wives) were asked informally whether do they have any scope or control on the income from sericulture. Whether respondents consider the view point of their wives or not, while taking some important decisions? Many women gave the response that they do exercise the control on income. While buying domestic purchases like clothes, utensils and permanent assets like land, gold and house site, women do exercise their control. Many women felt that without consulting them the husbands were not willing to proceed on any issue. It can be inferred that while decision making equal opportunity is existing among sampled households which is an indicater of modernization in socil relations.

Women not only participate in decision making process of household matters as well as in activities related to sericulture farming/cocoon rearing also. To elicit information, an opinion question is canvassed among the sampled respondents. The opinions are analysed and presented in Table 5.8.

Table 5.8 : Table Showing the Distribution of Respondents Opinion on Decision Making Process

Sl. No.	*Educational Status*	*Different Opinions*			*Total*
		Mutual	*Male dominates*	*Unilateral*	
1.	Illiterate	11 (21.57)	35 (68.63)	35 (9.80)	51 (100.0)
2.	Primary	60 (92.31)	5 (7.69)	---	65 (100.0)
3.	Middle	34 (100.0)	---	---	34 (100.0)
4.	SSC	27 (100.0)	---	---	27 (100.0)
5.	Higher Secondary	---	---	---	---

(Figures in Paranthesis indicate percentages).

The data revealed that 68.63% among illiterate respondents, the decision making process was dominated by male members. Whereas high percentage of respondents among primary, middle, SSC and higher secondary educated respondents, the decision making process was taking place on mutual understanding basis. The decision making process integrates when men and women are knowledgeble and capable.

Empowerment of Women

Theoritically, the concept of women's advancement in sericulture has a two fold implications. In the first instance, rural sericulturists have to be strengthened as producers in their own right using suitable interventions which help to increase their productivity and returns to their labour. In this instance women have to be reached with credit, access to resources viz., land, inputs, technology, training, information as well as the tools with which they can become viable producers in their own right. Such tools include group formation and leadership development; involvement in decision making on aspects of marketing and inputs, increasing women's access to sericulture income through savings. These steps will increase the empowerment of women's participation in sericulture as a viable economic activity, as producers, to the benefit of the family as well as sericulture sector in its entirety.

In the study area it was observed that many women irrespective of their caste were engaged in either feeding or picking up cocoons or changing beds for worms. Women belonging to weaker sections improved their status by participating in decision making and taking more modern course of action in critical situations. Women not only physically participating in different activities but mentally also assisting to their husbands and preparing children as good citizens.

Summing Up

In this chapter an effort has been made to understand the role of education in social change particularly among sericulturists. It is proved that education has played a major role in modernizing the entire gamut of issues and relations involved in sericulture. Education's impact has been proved in the framework of the tradition–modernity paradigm with stress on cultural change rather than structural change. Education has helped in inculcating modern values, attitudes and value–neutral thinking among the sampled respondents.

References

1. Allen R.Holmberg and Dobyns, Henry R–"The process of Accelerating Community Change", *Human Organization*, No.21, 1962.

2. Henry F.Dobyns–"The strategic Importance of Enlightenment and skill for power", *American Behavioural Science* No.8, 1965.

3. Daniel Lerner–The Passing of Traditional Society", *Modernizing the Middle East*, Free, 1958.

4. Philip, J.Foster–*Education and Social Change in Ghana*, Routledge, 1963.

5. Edward Shills–*The Intellectual between Traditions and Modernity: The Indian situation*, Mounton, 1961.

6. Schultz, T.W.–Investing in People : *The Economics of population quality*, University of California Press, USA, 1982.

7. Marion, J.Levy, JR–*Modernization and structure of societies*, princepton university press, New Jersey, 1966.

6

SUMMARY AND CONCLUSIONS

"Education will not cure all the problems of society, but without it no cure for any problem is possible."

— Johnson

The acquired capabilities of farm people play an important role in modernizing agriculture and also serve as means of production. Theoritically the level and distribution of the *inherited capabilities* tend to be more or less the same for large population. But the *acquired capabilities* are not given at any particular time frame. Although skills and related knowledge can be improved and enhanced throughout life, there are strong cultural and economic reasons for acquiring most of them while young. There is also the basic economic fact that acquired capabilities are not free; they entile real, identifiable costs. They are, in essence, an *investment in human capital.*

The term "human resources" is being used increasingly to take account of both the quantitative and qualitative attributes of workers whether they are skilled or unskilled, or function as managers, entrepreneures, planners and public administrators. Investment in education and training to increase the efficiency of people, is most important. But there are also other ways of investing in farm people, especially in adults who did not have an opportunity to attend school or if they did, it was all too little to have made them even effectively literate.

Education improves the productive capacity of societies and their political, economic and scientific institutions. It also helps reduce poverty by mitigating its effects on population, health and nutrition and by increasing the value and efficiency of the labour offered by the poor. As economies world wide are transferred by technological advances and new methods of production that depend on a well - trained and intellectually flexible labour force, education becomes even more significant.

The process of modern agricultural development focussed that the main difference between a traditional and a modern agriculture lies in the use of different factors of production: the former use traditional factors of production which have been in existance for a long time while the latter uses modern ones which keep changing in form as time goes by. Therefore, the problem of modern agricultural development is how to increase the supply of modern factors of production and how best farmers adopt and implement in their farms. This is possible through effective system of schooling and extension methods among the farmers.

The central argument for this study has set the stage that the *human capital* is a major source of economic and social development. Rapid sustained growth rests heavily on particular investments in farm people related to the new skills and knew knowledge that farm people must acquire to succeed for the high growth rate. A high level of skill is required in using new knowledge and modern input materials in mulberry cultivation and cocoon rearing. Therefore, it increases the quality of produce, and at the same time, increases yields of each crop and produces more per farm worker.

The modern complex pattern of production activities that characterize sericulture cultivation/ cocoon rearing has been made possible by two types of public investments.

i. Investment in research to discover and develop new practices and methods specifically tailored to the needs of farmers, and

ii. Investment in schooling not only of crops of specialists to extent this knowledge to farm people but of farm people themselves.

It is with this perspective of development process that the importance of education and training for modern agricultural development especially in sericulture is recognised and emphasised. In order to absorb new and scientific inputs and management skills in sericulture, well-educated manpower is necessary.

The study has been carried out with a holistic approach and interviewed 220 respondents of which 188 were sericulture cultivating/cocoon rearing farmers and remaining belonged to the category of non-cultivators. The methodology used in the study was intensive survey method and qualitative techniques. The basic variables studied were religion, educational status, occupational pattern, no.of layings reared per crop, annual income, level of knowledge about the mulberry plantation, awareness about the different aspects of cocoon rearing, knowledge about the different pests and diseases and possible remedies to control the situation etc.

Among the respondents, 30%, 55% and 14% belong to scheduled caste, backward class and other caste communities respectively. As far as educational status is concerned respondents belonging to Maluguru are having higher rate of educational percentage than Tumakunta respondents at all levels of education.

Based on the extent of land, respondents were categorised into less than one acre, less than two acre, less than five acre, and less than ten acre. There were about 55.9% and 14.0% respondents had less than 1 ac, 37.6% and 22.0% respondents having less than 2 ac, 1.2% and none respondents having less than 5ac and 5.3% and none respondents having less than 10 ac in the villages of Maluguru and Tumakunta respectively. About 54.7% of Maluguru farmers were rearing between one to three crops in a year. But in Tumakunta only 16% of farmers were rearing between one to three crops. About 40% and 5.3% of the respondents were rearing between 4 to 5 and above 6 crops in Maluguru respectively. Place of rearing is one of the important items while rearing silkworms. There were about 25.9% respondents having their own rearing shed, and about 52.9% respondents were rearing within their house and about 21.2% respondents were rearing in rented sheds at Maluguru. More or less similar pattern is found in Tumakunta as 4.0%, 20% and 2% were rearing in own shed, within the house and rented sheds respectively.

There were 5.9% respondents belonging to Maluguru village whose annual income is more than one lakh from sericulture. There were 41.8% respondents whose annual income from sericulture is less than Rs.6,000. And also there were 41.9% respondents whose annual income from sericulture is between Rs.6001 to 20,000. In the next highest category there were 9.4% respondents whose annual income is between 20,001 to one lakh. In comparision with Maluguru there were 10%, 22% and 4% respondents in Tumakunta whose income is falling under less than Rs.6,000; 6,001 to 20,000 and 20,001 to 40,000 respectively.

It is evident from the data that all respondents from Maluguru village were having either pucca or kutcha house. The percentage of respondents at Maluguru who occupied pucca houses were more than Tumakunta. The analysed data has been revealed that Malugure village respondents were better placed than Tumakunta respondents in possessing better basic social amenities.

Sericulture Industry : An overview

Silk is produced by silkworms through secretion of silk substance known as "Fibroin" covered with sericin a gummy substance and when it comes into contact with the air it gets solidified and becomes silk filament. The different types of leaves produce different varieties of silk. Nearly 70 percent of the silk proteins produced by a silkworm is directly derived from the proteins of the mulberry leaves. India is the only country where all the known four varieties of silk are produced.

Sericulture is a well established agro-based cottage industry. It is an effective tool for rural development as it generates income and employment. Out of the 5,76,000 villages in the country, sericulture is practised in about 50,000(8.7%) villages providing employment to the people belonging to weaker sections of the society including scheduled castes and scheduled tribes.

Andhra Pradesh is a mere speck on the sericulture map of India, during the start of the Vth Plan producing only around 300 tonnes of mulberry silk cocoons. Today she is the second largest producer of cocoons in the country, with an annual production of 30,000 tonnes and providing employment approximately to 10 lakh persons. In the year 1989 - 90, 11.7% belonging to scheduled caste, 7.7% belonging to scheduled tribe and 80.6% belonging to other caste families depend on this activity.

Educational Impact on Management of Mulberry Garden/Cocoon Rearing

Little empirical research has been carried out to understand the changes that are taking place in mulberry cultivation/cocoon rearing based on the educational status of sericulture farmers.

Education is an important element in management of sericulture. The individual gains through the reading skills, and he is able to extend the scope of his experience through the print media. One who can read and decode information is able to form generally favourable attitude towards new ideas as well as to specific technical information that he may consider and adopt. One might, therefore, expect those farmers with high print media exposure may have favourable attitude towards change, as well as greater technical know - how gained from such exposure. Education then becomes a catalyst of modernization by giving an individual access to media communication. The following diagram 6.1 illustrates the relationship of education to change/modernization variables through the intervening variables of print media exposure.

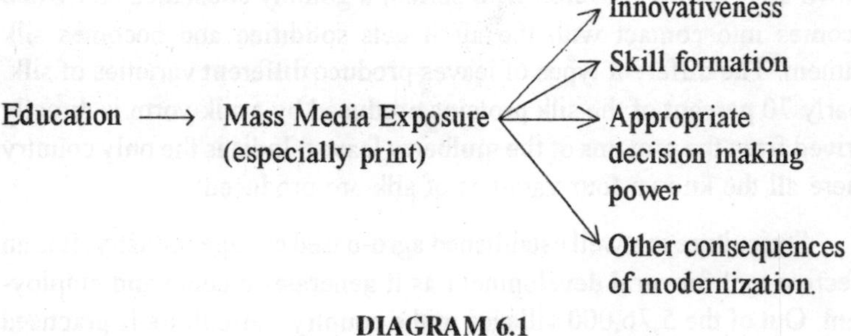

DIAGRAM 6.1

With the help of print media exposure the farmer would benefit *i*) control the rate of message input *ii*) store and retrieve print information from delayed use *iii*) key for unlocking more complex mental abilities.

Consequently, it is very useful and beneficial if the farmer is well aware of the high yielding varieties of mulberry cuttings. The data revealed that farmers who were educated upto primary and above standard were able to name some important varieties. Knowledge about the variety of mulberry planted was highly correlated with the educational level of the sericulturists since r value = .3127. Among illiterate cultivators the knowledge with regard to this item was very low.

Mulberry falls under the category of perennial crops and once it is properly planted and raised, it can come to full yielding capacity during the second year onwards. There is possibility of attacking diseases and pests and if the farmer is fully aware of different kinds of pests immediately it can be controlled. The knowledge among cultivators about the diseases and pests is very high. The analysis revealed that when the level of education increases the knowledge of pests and diseases also increases correspondingly.

Timely application and adequate doses of manure/fertilizer is an important item through which it would be possible to reap optimum quantity of leaf. With regard to use of manure and fertilizer for mulberry, the impact of education is found marginally significant. It is critical and important input on which future activities depend, no farmer can ignore this component.

It can be presumed that maximization of mulberry leaf yield per unit area will lead to the realization of two most important objectives namely increase cocoon production per acre and reduction in cost of production.

Educational Impact on Management of Silkworm Rearing

From time to time research/training institutes involved in the development of sericulture are propogating new technologies, seed varieties. To impart this new knowledge specific training modules prepared for the benefit of farmers. At the same time print media also actively played a role as catalyst. How far educate farmers can imbibe and implement the new methods of rearing technologies than the illiterate farmers is the prime concern of this part.

With regard to the number of disease free layings (dfls) the data revealed that 62.74% of illiterate cultivators were rearing less than 100 dfls. Very meagre 1.96% of illiterate farmers were able to reare beyond 200 dfls. According to the data, rearing beyond 200 dfls is possible only for the educated sericulturists. It was found positive correlation between education and number of dfls reared per crop.

The various technical aspects involved in rearing of silkworms like appropriate rearing house, importance of ventilation, optimum number of feeds, quality of leaves, disinfection of rearing shed, awareness of different diseases and possible measures to control the diseases are some of the important items examined.

With regard to rearing house a specific question was canvassed that what is the importance of more windows for rearing house. The data reveals that 5.89% among illiterate, 67.69% among primary, 97.06% among middle, 100% among SSC as well as higher secondary educated farmers stated correct answer. With regard to the environmental requirement the respondents knowledge was tested through the question that what should be the ceiling height of rearing shed. The percentage of correct answer was higher among educated farmers than the illiterate farmers.

Successful silkworm rearing depends more on technical and managerial manipulations. Enquiry on optimum atmoshpheric temperature - humidity conditions under which silkworms thrive best is rightly responded by 38.34% of primary, 67.65% of middle, 92.59% of S.S.C and 100.0% of higher secondary educated farmers. Another important aspect in rearing is rearing house as well as the appliances used in rearing should be invariably disinfect with 2% formalin prior to commencement of every rearing. The data revealed that 11.76%, 64.61%, 76.47%, 81.48% and 90.91% among illiterate, primary, middle, SSC and higher secondary educated farmers respectively were aware of the percentage of formalin to be used while disinfecting rearing house. None among the educated farmers gave incorrect answer. This type of knowledge is crucial input in controlling the spread of diseases effectively.

One of the pre-requisites for effective silkworm rearing is to maintain substantial standards of hygienic conditions to avoid pests and disease outbreak. In silkworm rearing, disease afflictions are rather serious and may occur total loss to the farmer. If the farmers have the knowledge and skill of identifying diseases carefully, they can adopt controlling measures immediately. The data revealed that among primary educated farmers 61.54%, among middle 85.29%, among SSC 92.59% and among higher secondary 100.0% were aware of all important seasonal diseases. It can also be deduced from the data that awareness about diseases is steadly increasing with the increase in educational level.

It is not only important to have knowledge about various diseases but also knowledge about medicine and symptoms of the diseases. Based on the data, farmers who were educated upto higher secondary level aware of the medicine for all important seasonal diseases cent percent. It is infered that educated farmers can be a better managers in crisis rather than illiterate farmers. It was also found that there is a strong association between the variables since its *r* value = .3127.

The ultimate aim of any producer is to get more production and more income. The data with regard to crop-wise cocoon production per annum has been collected from farmers and computed the productivity per 100 disease free layings. The cocoon productivity range of 21 - 40 kg was attained 41.18% among illiterate, 80.0% among primary, 85.29% among middle, 59.26% among SSC and 27.27% among higher secondary educated farmers. In addition to this the data proved that the highest cocoon productivity 41–50 kgs is possible only to educated farmers. The increase in productivity of the farmers proved that education played a very crucial role in management/manipulate the process of cocoon rearing. It was also found that strong correlation existed between the variables since r value = .2703.

After analysing the productivity a proximate outcome of education, income a perceptible variable, is measured as the efficiency of cultivators who are managers of the activity. The data revealed that 66.67% of illiterate cultivators were getting Rs.6000/- annual income which is at the minimum level. Highest income level i.e., Rs.1 lakh and above was not possible to any of the illiterate farmer. Whereas 1.54%, 5.88%, 14.8% and 27.27% primary, middle, SSC and higher secondary educated farmers respectively were earning highest level of income. The data further suggest that there is a high correlation between education and income since its r value = .6230.

Education and Social Change

Hardly anything in our midst is static. Everything changes, every organism grows, every life flows. The society composed of human beings also undergoes changes. These changes occur in its cultural pattern, in its structure and consequently on its members. This process of change is quite complicated and needs a careful and deep understanding.

Education is considered as the most powerful instrument of social change. It is through education that the society can bring desirable changes and modernise itself. Education is the most important prime mover for not only economic development but also bring social change. The knowledge, skills and values acquired through education not only meet the economic needs of society, but they are also permeated with a social content.

The relation between education and social change has been examined in rural contexts, where rigid class systems have proved barriers to education as well as agricultural changes. A study by Lerner was found that the key to modernisation lies in the participant society, that is, one in which people go through school, read news papers, participate politically through elections and change opinions on matters to note that literacy not only proved to be key variable in moving from a traditional to a transitional society but also the pivotal agent in the transition to a fully participant society.

The main aim in the issue of education and social change is to understand the influence of education on social issues like change in values, beliefs, attitudes and modernisation among sericulturists. The source for this empirical analysis is the selected respondents as well as my personal observation. The issues examined here are modernisation in values and beliefs, demographic aspects, health and nutritional issues, social mobility, social relations, decision making process and empowerment of women.

Education is considered to be the main instrument of change in social sphere and change was visualised in the framework of the *traditon-modernity paradigm*, with stress on the *cultural* rather than on the *structural* change.

Impact of education among respondents has been analysed in terms of changes in beliefs and values which play a critical role in the development of individual and society. Sericulturists while cultivating mulberry as well as cocoon rearing observe many customs and traditions. A woman in her menstruation period should not enter into the rearing house as well as is not allowed to feed the worms etc. Like this there are innumerable sentimetns and beliefs prevalent in the minds of farmers. The level of education on these beliefs and values is inversely correlated. Education played a decisive role in inculcating positive thinking in modernising beliefs and values.

The demographic aspects were also examined among sericulturists. Many educated sericulturists formed positive opinion about the small family norm. In addition to positive attitude towards small family norm, farmers were having knowledge about the different types of birth control methods. The data were revealed that 73.85% of primary, 97.06% of middle, 100.0% of SSC as well as higher secondary educated farmers understood the importance of small family norm and other related benefits.

The phenomenon of social mobility was observed among the sampled respondents. The horizontal social mobility has taken place more among the scheduled castes and backward class respondents. Education helped the farmers to take up the modern activity and increased their household earnings. Many households among thesse communities had reduced their dependency on agriculture labour market. Now the status has changed from agricultural wage earners to sericulture entrepreneur.

The concept of modernisation in social relations among respondents is verified based on the respondents opinion on different issues. Practice of discrimination and untouchability is common phenomenan even today in some rural areas. Due to the spread of education and impact of industrialisation the problem of untouchability and other related purity - pollution concepts have drastically reduced. The main factors responsible for modern thinking are (i) rationalisation of traditional values (ii) recognition of human dignity and (iii) change in thinking pattern. All these modern values have emerged and developed due to the spread of education.

This fact was also corroborated during my personal observation, when few of twice-born status respondents who were rearing worms in rented sheds, belonging to the scheduled castes community, without any inhibition used to go to SC basti and rear their worms. Neighbours, mostly small and marginal scheduled caste farmers, used to visit the sheds and try to make a suggestion. In this process the reciprocity and interaction used to take place cutting across the caste barriers. This may be a stray case but this lends support to the fact that caste restrictions are declining.

In the study area it was observed that many women, irrespective of their caste, were engaged in either feeding or picking up cocoons or changing beds for worms. Women belonging to weaker sections improved their status by participating in decision making and taking more modern course of action in critical situations. Women not only are physically participating in different activities but also assisting to their husbands and preparing children as good citizens.

It can be concluded that educated respondents who were able to decode the existing information and make use in rearing practices got benefited by increasing productivity and production of cocoons. Ultimately this process led to more income for farmers. Due to this improved quality of life they got opportunity to spare children for education which was again an essential part in *human capital formation.*

Therefore, the objectives of the study set for enquiry is greatly accomplished as the findings reveal that there is a positive association and significant correlation between education and economic development as well social change among the sericulturists.

Bibliography

Abdul Aziz and Hanumappa, H.G.—*Silk Industry: Problems and Prospects,* Ashish Publishing House, New Delhi, 1985.

Adamski, I—"Improved peasant Farming as a Result of the Social and Professional Activities of the Farmers", *International Journal of Agrarian Affairs,* Vol.V, No.4, July 1969.

Adiseshiah, M.S—"Education and Development" in Readings in *Economics of Education,* UNESCO, Paris, 1968.

Ahmed, M and Coombs, P—*Education for Rural Development,* Praeger Publishers, New York, 1977.

Alex Inkeles and David Smith H.—*Becoming Modern: Individual Change in Six Developing Countries,* Massachusetts, Harvard University Press, London, 1974.

Allen R.Holmberg and Dobyns, Henry F—"The Process of Accelerating Community Change", *Human Organization,* (21), 1962.

Alva Myrdal—"The Power of Education" in *Education in World Perspective* (ed) by Emmet John Hughes, Lancer Books, New York, 1965.

Anderson, C.A and Bowman, M.J—*Education and Economic Development*, Chicago, 1965.

Arthur Lewis, W—*The Theory of Economic Growth,* Richard D.Irrwin, *Inc. Homewood*, Illinois, U.S.A, 1955.

Becker, G.S—*Human Capital : A Theoritical and Empirical Analysis with Special Reference to Education*, National Bureau of Educational Research, New York, 1964.

Beeby, C.E—*Quality of Education in Developing Countries*, Harvard University Press, Cambridge, 1966.

Benson, C.S—*The School and Economic System*, Foundation of Education Series, Chicago, 1966.

——————, *The Economics of Public Education*, Houghton Nifflin, Boston, 1968.

Bhagawati, J—"Education, Class Structure and Income Equality", *World Development*, 1/5 (May), 1973.

Bhatia, S.C and Gupta, N.P (Eds)—*Linking Literacy with Development*, Indian Adult Association, New Delhi, 1980.

Blaug, M—*An Introduction to the Economics of Education*, The Penguin, London, 1968.

———, Economics of Education—*Selected Annotated Bibliography*, Pergamon Press, Oxford, 1978.

Bowman, M.J—"Social Returns to Education", *International Social* Science *Journal*, 14/4, 1962.

—————, "The Human Investment Revolution in Economic Thought", *Sociology of Education*, 39/2 (Spring), 1966.

Bowman, M.J et.al—*Readings in Economics of Education*, UNESCO, Paris, 1968.

Bowman, M.J—Concerning the role of Education, cited in the *Human Investment in Economic thought* (Eds.) by Mark Blaug.

Bowen, W.G.—*Economic Aspects of Education: Three Eassys*, Princeton Industrial Relations Centre, Princeton, 1963.

Bowles, S and Ginits, H—"The Problem of Human Capital Theory : A Marxian Critique", *American Economic Review*, 65/2, May (Papers & Proceedings), 1975.

Chandra Reddy, Y—*The Impact of Formal Education on Agricultural Income in Andhra Pradesh*, Unpublished Ph.D Thesis, Osmania University, Hyderabad, 1987.

Charles, K. V. and Paniker, P.G.K—"Education and Economic Development—A Case Study of Kerala", *Development Digest*, January, 1968.

Charsely, S.R—*Culture and Sericulture: Social Anthropology and Development in a South Indian Livestock Industry*, Academic Press, London, 1982.

Chatterjee, Rachel—*Credit Tie-up : The A.P. Experience*, Commissionarate of Sericulture, Hyderabad.

Chaudhri, D.P.—*Education and Agricultural Productivity in India*, Ph.D Thesis, Delhi University, Delhi, 1968.

——————, *Education in Production and Modernizing Agriculture in Asian Underdeveloped Countries—Structural Re-Adjustment in Asian Perspective*, Japan Economic Research Centre, Vol.I, No.17, Tokyo, 1971.

——————, *Education Innovations and Agricultural Development*, Croom Helm, London, 1979.

Chitnis, S—"Higher Education and the Scheduled Castes", *Journal of Higher Education*, 1/2 (Autumn), 1975.

Christopher, Colclough—"Primary Schooling and Economic Development : A Review of Evidence", World Bank Staff Working paper, World Bank, Washington D.C, 1980.

Clough, C and Hallak—*Some Issues in Rural Education, Efficiency and Employment*, UNESCO, Paris, 1975.

Cohen, E—*The Economics and Education*, Health exington Books, 1972.

Correa, H—*The Economics of Human Resources*, North Holland Publishing Co., Amesterdam, 1963.

Coombs, Philip H with Roy Prosser and Manzoor Ahmed—*New Paths to Learning for Rural Children and Youth*, UNICEF, International Council for Educational Development, New York, 1973.

Coombs, P.H.—*The World Crisis in Education. The view from Eightees*, Oxford Press, New York, 1985.

Cotlear, Daniel—"Farmer Education and Farm Efficiency in Peru : The Role of Schooling, Extension Services and Migration", EDT Discussion Paper 49, *World bank*, Washington D.C, 1986.

Daniel, Lerner—"The Passing of Traditional Society", *Modernizing the Middle East*, Free, 1958.

D' Arth, R—*Education and Development in the Third World*, Health Laxington Book, 1975.

Davis, R.G—*Planning Education for Development*, Cambridge, 1980.

Deb, K—*Rural Development in India Since Independence*, Sterling, New Delhi, 1986.

Debeauvais, M—"The Concept of Human Capital", *International Social Science Journal*, XV, 1962.

Denison, Edward F—*Why Growth Rates Differ*? The Brookings Institution, Washington D.C.

Dobb, M—*Some Aspects of Economic Development*, Delhi School of Economics, Delhi, 1957.

Shills—*The Intellectual between Traditions and Modernity* : *The Indian Situation*, Mouton, 1961.

Eisemon, Thomas O; John Schwille and Robert Prouty—*Empirical Results and Conventional Wisdom*, in Strategies for increasing Primary School Effectiveness in Burundi, Mimeo, 1989.

Evenson, R.E et. al—*Agricultural Research and Productivity*, New Heaven, 1975.

F.A.O—*Manuals on Sericulture*, Agricultural Bulletins, Food and Agricultural Organization of the United Nations, Rome, 1978.

Foster, P and Sheffield, J.R—*Education and Rural Development, World Year Book of Education*, Even Bros, London, 1974.

Galbraith, J.K—*Economic Development in Perspective*, Harvard University Press, Cambridge, 1962.

Gingberg, E—*Human Resource : The Wealth of Nation*, Simmon & Schuster, New York, 1968.

Gisser, M—"Schooling and the Farm Problem" *Econometrica*, Vol.33, No.3, July, 1965.

Goel, S.C—*Education and Economic Growth in India*, Delhi, Macmillan,

1975.

Gopinathan Nair, P.R—*Primary Education,Population Growth and Socio-Economic Change : A Comparative Study with Particular Reference to Kerala*, Allied Publications, New Delhi, 1981.

Government of India—*The First Five Year Plan, 1951—56*, Planning Commission, New Delhi, 1952.

——————, *Education and National Development*, The Report of Education Commission 1964—66, G.O.I, New Delhi, 1964.

——————, *The Seventh Five Year Plan, 1980—85*, Vol.I, Planning Commission, GOI, New Delhi, 1985.

——————, *Challenge of Education : A Policy Perspective*, Ministry of Human Resource Development, New Delhi, 1985.

——————, *National Policy on Education*, Ministry of Human Resource Development, New Delhi, 1986.

Govinda, R—*School Education in Rural Areas,* Baroda Society for Education Research and Development, Baroda, 1981.

Griffiths, V.L—*Problems of Rural Education,* IIEP, UNESCO, Paris 1972.

Griliches, Zvi—"The Sources of Measured Productivity Growth in U.S. Agriculture 1940—1960", *Journal of Political Economy*, Vol.LXXI, No.4, 1963.

Habte, A; Psacharopoulas, G and Heyneman, S.P—*Education and Development,* World bank, Washington D.C, 1983.

Hadimani, R.N et.al—"Sericulture As a Leverage of Social Mobility Among Scheduled Castes in Rural Areas", *Journal of Institute of Economic Growth,* 20 (1&2), 1985.

Hajela, P.D—"Investment in Education—A Point of View", in Pandit, H.N. (Eds), *NCERT,* New Delhi, 1969.

Hallak, J—*Educational Costs and Productivity,* UNESCO, IIEP, Paris, 1967.

Hansen, W.Lee—*Education, Income and Human Capital,* Columbia University Press, 1970.

Hanson, J.W. et.al—*Education and Development of Nations,* New York, 1966.

Hanumappa, M.G—*Sericulture for rural Development,* Himalaya Publishing House, Delhi, 1986.

Harbison, F.H—*Human Resource and The Wealth of Nations,* Oxford University Press, London, 1973.

Harbison, F.H & Myers, C—*Education, Manpower and Economic Growth,* Mc Graw, London, 1964.

Harker, Bruce Rogers—*Education Communication and Agricultural Changes—A Study of Japanese Farmers,* Unpublished Ph.D Thesis, University of Chicago, Chicago, 1971.

——————"The Contribution of Schooling to Agricultural Modernization", Foster and Sheffield (Eds), *World Year Book of Education,* 1973.

Hauser, R.M.—"Socio-Economic Background and Differential Returns to Education", *Solman L.C & Taubman P.J (Eds),* 1973.

Hayami, Y and Ruttan, V.W—Agricultural Productivity Differences among countries", *American Economic Review,* December, 1970.

Henery, F.Dobyns—"The Strategic Importance of Enlightenment and Skill for Power", *American Behavioural Science,* (8), 1965.

Horvat, B—"The Optimum Rate of Investment", *Economic Journal,* 68/282, December, 1958.

Huffman, Walace—*The Contribution of Education and Extension to Differential Rates of Change,* Unpublished Ph.D Thesis, Department of Economics, University of Chicago, Chicago, 1972.

Husain, I.Z—"Returns to Education in India", in *Singh Baljit (ed),* 1967.

Illich, I—*Deschooling Society,* Calder & Boyars, London, 1971.

Indian Constitution—*Government of India,* New Delhi, 1950.

Indian National Commission—*Government of India,* New Delhi, 1966.

Jamison, D.T and Lau, L—*Farmer Education and Farm Efficiency,* The John Hopkins University Press, London, 1983.

Jamison, Dean and Peter Mock—"Farmer Education and Farm Efficiency in Nepal : The Role of Schooling, Extension Services and Cognitive Skills", *World Development,* (12), 1984.

Joshi, P.C' and Rao, M.R—"Social and Economic Factors in Literacy Education in India", *Economic Weekly,* 16(1), 4, 1964.

Kiker, B.F—"The Concept of Human Capital in the History of Economic Thought", *Journal of Political Economy,* 1967.

——————, *Investment in Human Capital,* University of Carolina, Columbia, 1971.

Kneller, G.F—*Education and Economic Thought,* John Wiley, New York, 1968.

Kothari, Rajani—*Education and National Development,* Report of the Education Commission, Government of India, New Delhi, 1966.

Kothari, V.N—"Returns to Education in India", in *B.Singh (Ed.),* 1967.

Kothari, V.N and Panchamukhi, P.R—"Economics of Education. A Trend Report", in D.T.Lakdawala (Ed.), *A Survey of Research in Economics:* Vol.6, Allied Publishers, New Delhi, 1980.

Krishna Swamy, S—*New Technology of Silkworm Rearing,* Central Silk Board (Reprinted from Bulletin No.2 of the CSR & TI, Mysore) Bangalore, 1990.

Kurien John—*Elementary Education in India: Myth, Reality and Alternatives,* Vikas, New Delhi, 1983.

Kuznets, S—"Trends in Capital Formation", *UNESCO,* REED, 1968.

Lewis, W.A—"Education and Economic Development" Readings in Economics of Education, *UNESCO,* 1968.

Lockheed, M.E., Jamison, D.T and Lau, L.J—"Farmer Education and Farm Efficiency : A Survey", *Economic Development and Cultural Change"* 29/1 October, 1980.

Lockheed, Marlaine, E., John Middleton and Greeta Nettleton (eds)—"Educational Technology : Sustainable and Effective use". Education and Employment Background Paper PHREEY/91/32, *World Bank,* Washington D.C, 1991.

Machlup, F—*The Production and Distribution of Knowledge in United States,* Princeton, New Jersey, 1962.

Majumdar, Vina—*Education and Social Change,* Indian Institute of Advanced Study, Shimla, 1972.

Malassis, L—*The Rural World Educational Development,* Crown Helms, London, 1976.

Malhotra, P.C and Minocha, C—"Capital Formation in Human Resources through Education", *Kothari, V.N. (Ed.),* 1965.

Manocha, L and Sharma, H—"Levels of Human Resource Development in the states of India", *Manpower Journal,* 15/3, (Oct—Dec), 1979.

Marion J.Levy, Jr—*Modernization and Structure of Societies,* Princetion University Press, New Jersery, 1966.

Marshall, A—*The Principles of Economics,* Macmillian, Book—IV, 1890.

Mathur, S.S—*A Sociological Approach to Indian Education,* Vinod Pustak Mandir, Agra, 1985.

Mazumdar—"On the Economics of Relative Efficiency of Small Farmers", *Economic Weekly* (Special Number), 1983.

Mc Clelland, David, C—*The Achieving Society,* The Free Press, New York Collier, Macmillan Ltd, London, 1961.

Mellor, J.W—"The use and productivity of Farm Family Labour in Early Stages in Agricultural Development", *Journal of Farm Economics* (August) 1963.

__________, *The Economics of Agricultural Development,* Cornell University Press, Ithaca, 1966.

Millikan, Max F—"Education for innovation", in *Restless Nations : A Study of World Tensions and Development,* Dodd, Mead & Company, New York, 1962.

Morgan, J and David, M—"Education and Income", *Quarterly Journal of Economics,* 77/3 (August), 1963.

Muthayya, B.C and Vijaya Kumar, S—*Psycho-Social Dimensions of Agricultural Development,* National Institute of Rural Development, Hyderabad, 1980.

Myinth, H—"Investment in Social Transformation" in Mier, C.M (Ed), *Leading Issues in Development Economics*, New York, 1964.

————,—"Education and Economic Development", *Social and Economic Studies* (March), 1965.

Myrdal, G—*Asian Drama : An Inquiry into the Poverty of Nations*, Pantheon, New York, Vol.III, 1968.

Nalla Goundan, A.M—*Education and Development : A Study of Human Capital Formation and its Role in in Economic Development in India*, Ph.D Thesis, Kurukshetra University, Kurukshetra, 1965.

————, "Investment in Education in India", in *Hansen (Ed.)*, 1967.

Nautiyal, K.C—*Education and Rural Poor*, Commonwealth Publishers, New Delhi, 1979.

————, "Investment Shyness in Elementary Education", *Indian Journal of Education*, NCERT, New Delhi, 1979.

Nautiyal, K.C and Sharma, Y.D—*Equalization of Educational Opportunities for Scheduled Castes and Scheduled Tribes*, NCERT, New Delhi, 1979.

Nautiyal, K.C—"Women Education and Rural Development", Paper Presented at National Seminar on Education for Rural Development, *Indian Institute of Education*, Pune (Mimeo), 1982.

Nelson, R.R and Phelps, E—"Investment in Humans, Technology, Diffusion and Economic Growth", *American Economic Review*, May, 1966.

Operational Research Group—Family Planning Practices in India. *The First All India Survey Report*, Baroda, 1979.

Panchamukhi, P.R—"Investment in Human Beings: A New Dimension to the Theory of Capital", *Indian Economic Journal*, (April—June), 1966.

————, "Educational Capital in India", *Indian Economic Journal*, 12/3 (January—March), 1985.

Panikar, P.G.K—"Resources not the constraint on Health Improvement : A Case Study of Kerala", in the *Economic and Political Weekly*, Vol.XIV, No.44, November, 1979.

Pareek, U—*Education and Rural Development in Asia*, New Delhi, 1982.

Parnes, H.S (Eds.)—*Planning Education for Economic and Social Development,* OECD, Paris, 1964.

Philip, J. Foster—*Education and Social Change in Ghana,* Routledge, 1963.

Phillips, H.M—*Literacy and Development,* UNESCO, Paris, 1970.

Psacharopoulos, G—*Returns to Education,* Jossey—Bass Inc. San Francisco., 1973.

————, "Education as an Investment", in *Education and Development,* News from World Bank, 1983.

Prakash, B—*Education and Rural Development,* National Institute of Educational Planning and Administration (Mimeo), 1984.

Rao, V.K.R.V—*Education and Human Resource Development,* Allied Publishers, New Delhi, 1961.

Rati, Ram—"Role of Education in Production: A slightly New Approach", *Quarterly Journal of Economics",* Vol.95, No.2, September, 1980.

Rogers, E.M.—*Modernization Among Peasants: The Impact of Communication,* Holt, Rinehart and Winston, INC., New York, 1969.

Rostow, W.W—*The Stages of Economic Growth,* Cambridge University Press, Cambridge, 1960.

Rudolph, S.H and Rudolph, L.I (Eds.)—*Education and Politics in India,* Oxford University Press, Delhi, 1972.

Schultz, T.W—*The Theory of Economic Development,* Cambridge, 1951.

—————, "Capital Formation by Education", *Journal of Political Economy,* December,1960.

——————, *The Economic value of Education,* Columbia University Press, New York, 1963.

——————, *Transforming Traditional Agriculture,* New Heaven, yale University Press, London, 1964.

——————, "Investment in Human Capital", in *Economics of Education* (Eds.) by M.Blung, Vol. I English Language Book Society and Penguin Books, 1968.

————————, "Investment in Education : The Equity—Efficiency quandary", *Journal of Political Economy,* 80/3 (May—June), Supplement, 1972.

————————, *The Economics of Being Poor,* Nobel Lecture, Nobel Foundation, Stockholm, 1979.

————————, *Investing in People : The Economics of population quality,* University of California, 1981.

Schumacher, E.F—*Small is Beautiful,* New Delhi, 1977.

Schumpeter, J.A—*History of Economic Analysis,* New York, 1954.

Scribner, Sylvia and Michael Cole—*The Psychology of Literature,* Massachussetts, Harvard University Press, Cambridge, 1981.

Sharan, Tripurari—*Sericulture and Silk Industry : A Study in quest of Appropriate Technology,* Consortium on Rural Technology, Delhi, 1984.

Singh, A.K—*Differential Impact of Education, Industrialization and Urbanization onModernity,* Center for International Affairs, Harvard University Press, Cambridge, 1968.

Singh, S.N—*Industrialization in Modern Perspective,* Classical Publications, New Delhi, 1979.

Silkman's Companion—Central Silk Board, Bangalore, 1989.

Sinha, D—*Indian Villages in transition : A Motivational Analysis,* Associated Publishing House, New Delhi, 1969.

Smith, Adam—*The Wealth of Nations,* London, 1776.

Smith, T.L—*Sociology of Rural Life,* Harper , New York, 1947.

Som P. Pudasaini—The Effects of Education in Agriculture : Evidence from Nepal", *American Journal of Agricultural Economics,* Vol.65, No.3, August, 1983.

Statistical Biennial—*Silk in India,* Central Silk Board, Bangalore, 1992.

Streeten, P.P—"Economic Development and Education" Hufner et.al (Eds.) *Economics of Education,* 1969.

Strumilin, S.G—"The Economic significance of People's Education", cited in Huq, M.S. *Education, Manpower and Development in South and South—East Asia,* 1924.

Tang, A.M.—"Research and Education in Japanese Agricultural Development 1880—1938", *Economic Studies Quarterly,* Vol.XIII, Feb—May, 1963.

Todaro, M.P—*Economic Development in the Third World* , Longman, New York, 1977.

UNESCO—*Investment in Education : Regional Technical Assistance,* Seminar on Investment in Education, Paris, 1967.

UNESCO—*Readings in Economic Education,* Paris, 1964.

UNO—*Poverty, Unemployment and Development Policy : A Case Study of Selected Issues with Reference to Kerala,* New York, 1975.

UNICEF—*Assignment Children,* No.49/50, Geneva, Spring, 1980.

Venkatasubramanian, K—*Education and Economic Development in India : Tamil Nadu—A Case Study,* Frank Bros, Delhi, 1980.

Warren C. Baum—*Investing in Development : Lessons of World Bank Experience,* World Bank, Oxford University Press, New York, 1985.

Welch, F—"Education and Production", *Journal of Political Economy,* Vol.78, No.1, Jan—Feb, 1970.

Welch, E—"Relationship between Income and schooling", in Kerlinger F. et.al. (Eds.) *Review of Research in Education,* Illions, 1974.

Wharton, Jr.C.R—"Education and Agricultural Growth . The Role of Education in the early State Agriculture" cited in Anderson, C.A and Bowman, M.J (Eds.), *Education and Economic Development,* Aldine Press, Chicago, 1965.

World Bank—*Education Sector Policy Paper,* Washington D.C, 1980.

——————, *World Development Report,* World Bank, Washington D.C. 1980.

Wykstra, R.A—*Education and Economics of Human Capital,* The Free Press, New York, 1971.

Yadava, J.S—"Mass Media and Social Change in India", *Social Change,* June—Sep, Nos. 2 & 3, Vol. 16. 1980.

INDEX